DJ BBQ

FIRE FOOD

THE ULTIMATE BBQ COOKBOOK

Photography by David Loftus

Hardie Grant

QUADRILLE

— CONTENTS —

WELCOME TO FIRE FOOD

Yes! You have arrived – welcome to my live fire book. Greetings. I am here to help you with your next BBQ cookout.

For those of you who aren't familiar with my work on YouTube, my name is Christian Stevenson, aka DJ BBQ. I've been cooking BBQ since I was six years old and made it a full-time job in 2012 when I started my 'catertainment' company, DJ BBQ. During the summer, my crew and I build a restaurant and soundsystem on the festival circuit. We slow-cook pork shoulder, grill the best burgers and spit-roast entire beef legs (top bit), all over live fire. It's a proper smörgåsbord of delicious BBQ and tasty tunes. We cook beats and meats – that's catertainment. I also produce online content to complement the live vibes. Every other week, I upload a fresh BBQ recipe onto my YouTube channel. So if you find you have any questions about these recipes, or need more inspiration, the chances are you'll find some help on my video channel.

The whole reason I do this fun and exhausting occupation is that food tastes better cooked over fire. It's the lost ingredient. Plus, being outdoors is way better. Fresh air, good friends, great tunes, a crackling fire and, of course, cold beers. That's all that's needed.

We've been cooking on gas and electricity for more than a century. Before this, cooking was mostly done over live fire, and in many parts of the world live fire remains the dominant method for cooking. Yeah, that's right, BBQ is how it all started. Once there was fire, there was progression. There was evolution. Fire allowed us to masticate and digest food with way more ease, and our brains developed because of it. Fire and food helped the evolution of mankind.

These days, we stay indoors and work with the convenience of other heat sources. But what we are missing is a key ingredient that comes from the combustion of fuel. When we cook on wood, something dynamic happens. The smoke and gases that emanate from the wood give our food another layer of flavour. The sweet wood notes permeate the BBQ, awakening our tastebuds to the upper echelons of awesome!

Handling fire and heat is a job in itself. That's why most people turn a dial and stick their joint of meat in the oven thinking, they're going to get roast beef. It is not roast beef. It is baked beef, and it is nowhere near as good as kissing that joint with a lick of live fire. Handling live fire is one of the best skills a human can possess.

I've been walking the Earth for almost 50 years. I've travelled extensively throughout South and Central America, Pakistan, Lebanon, Europe, the Baltics, Australasia and Northern Africa. I've watched locals handle live fire and achieve incredible results from their ancient techniques. I've been watching chefs, gauchos, artisans, pitmasters and home cooks from all over this planet cook BBQ and I have soaked up many of their techniques and recipes.

In this book I will show you a plethora of grilling, roasting and smoking techniques. There's a slew of tasty recipes, covering meat, seafood, veggies, fruits and some wonderful little surprises. We are going to goof-proof your cooking so you can feel confident rocking your grill.

Your cookouts will never be the same again!

ALCHEMY OF FIRE

People often ask me the same question, 'Charcoal or gas?' My response is normally, 'What's the point in going outdoors if you're cooking on gas? There's a perfectly good gas burner in your kitchen.' BBQ starts with fuel: that means lump wood charcoal (which I also call coals or charcoal), seasoned wood chunks, and even charcoal briquettes. Learning about fuel is the best place to start...

As a child, I learned how to cook BBQ on my dad's gas grill. But, as soon as I fled the nest at the tender age of 18, I bought my first proper cooker, a Weber 18-Inch Kettle. My life in BBQ changed forever. Then I bought three Lang offset firebox cookers and things got really exciting. Then I met the premier charcoal maker from the UK, Matt Williams of Oxford Charcoal Company, who has spent over 25 years working with wood – 20 years as a thatcher and 7 as a charcoal maker. Matt tours with the DJ BBQ crew on the summer festival circuit and we cook on his fuel and learn what his fuel does to our BBQ – essentially, amazing things!

FORGET GAS

Most backyard enthusiasts use one of three cooking fuels: charcoal, gas or wood. But not many people understand the differences and especially the positive benefits of using charcoal and wood over gas.

We never work with gas. You can make a gas grill better by getting rid of the gas in the canister and throwing a bunch of wood or charcoal in there instead.

There is no flavour in gas. Wood and charcoal add flavour, but gas is a hydrocarbon, so when you burn it, you make a lot of water. By using gas to cook meat, you're essentially broiling the meat and not properly searing it to get that beautiful Maillard reaction. That luscious steak crust that most pitmasters are looking for can only truly come from a charcoal fire.

THE BEAUTY OF CHARCOAL

Charcoal gives off a radiant heat that is more controllable than almost anything. It can be used to smelt iron, slow-cook a brisket or grill a steak. The only difference is airflow. The temperature is regulated entirely by the amount of oxygen you give the charcoal. This is the reason why people have been making wood into charcoal for over 30,000 years. Without it, we couldn't have had the bronze age, or the iron age – and you wouldn't have an iPhone. It's the original industrial fuel and it's one of the most controllable fuels you will cook on. But you need to get to know your fuel if you're going to cook your food on it.

One of the reasons many people opt for gas over charcoal is that people claim they can cook straight away on gas compared with charcoal. I tell them, 'I can have hot coals quicker than you can preheat your gas grill.' Fact. I will have a hotter heat using proper charcoal within 6 minutes – and that's 5 minutes faster than a gas grill (see How to Light Your Charcoal on page 11).

WHAT IS CHARCOAL?

Charcoal is the product of thermal destructive distillation of anything that used to be alive. You can make charcoal out of many different things, from bones to cow manure. We generally use wood – although we have experimented. We've made decent charcoal from the blade bones from pork shoulder, but you need a lot of them to really get things cooking.

The thermal destructive distillation process uses heat to break apart all the components of wood. This form of distillation changes solid matter into vapours and gases (wood smoke). Only the underlying carbon structure will survive this process, so what you're left with is lump wood charcoal. Wood would usually catch fire when heated, but when you take away the oxygen in order to allow combustion, it will only produce smoke. So to efficiently make charcoal, one needs to heat the wood but also starve it of oxygen.

MAKING CHARCOAL

Oxford Charcoal Company's Matt Williams says, 'There are millions of ways to create charcoal, it's just that my way is the best.' Matt recycles all the smoke given off from the heated charcoal wood (which is smoking rather than on fire) back into the kiln furnace to keep heating the charcoal wood. So he just recycles the heat to cook the charcoal, which makes the kiln almost self-sustaining, only requiring a relatively small amount of additional fuel during the burn. This is the cleanest and most environmentally friendly way of making charcoal.

Like cooking BBQ, making charcoal is about temperature and time. If you cook wood at a very high temperature you are creating pure carbon with little flavour. If you cook that wood at a lower temperature for a long time, you are still creating charcoal but it retains the properties that give off wood note flavours when it is used in a cooker. The main property left in the charcoal is lignin, which is a complex organic polymer. When the lignin burns, it mostly creates alkaloids and these alkaloids contain nitrogen, and nitrous oxide is produced. It is the nitrous oxide produced in the burn that reacts with the meat and gives your BBQ that pink colour or 'smoke ring'. Gas doesn't do this.

SINGLE SPECIES VS MIXED-SPECIES CHARCOAL

The beauty of a single species charcoal is the clarity of flavour. Each species will have a subtle influence on the flavour of your BBQ. The sweet nuttiness of chestnut charcoal lends itself to white meats and fish, while the darker, heavier flavour of wild cherry charcoal will stand up against a stronger flavoured meat, like venison. Experiment and you'll find your own favourites, and begin using charcoal as an ingredient.

Flavour is a great bonus from using a single species but the real advantage is the controllability. All well made charcoal will have the same amount of energy per kilogram; what makes the difference is the structure of the charcoal. Oak charcoal has an open structure and burns fast and hot. Birch charcoal has a very closed and compact structure so it burns slowly and at a lower temperature. Beech charcoal is a lovely consistent charcoal – it burns well and is great for keeping the fire low and slow. That is the beauty of a single species charcoal: once you get to understand how it burns, it's easier to control your cooking temperature.

When you cook on mixed-species charcoal, you will lose a bit of that predictability and controllability, as the charcoal may burn a little hotter in places and a little cooler in others. The main thing to remember is controlling the airflow into your cooker. With a little thought, you should be able to keep your charcoal burning at the required temperature.

SHOP-BOUGHT CHARCOAL

Most charcoal bought from the high street will be made from unsustainable wood. It will probably be mixed species and may contain other ingredients apart from wood. It will burn differently from bag to bag, and you may even find that it smells of more like paraffin than wood when it's burning. This is often due to chemicals added to the charcoal in an attempt to make it burn better. These chemicals will taint your food and make the whole experience unpleasant. To tell you the truth, If my only choice of fuel is charcoal covered in instant lighting paraffin, then I'd opt for a gas grill.

Try to use a local sustainable charcoal supplier. Search out your local charcoal-makers and wood suppliers. Ask where the fuel has come from and who has made the charcoal. Here in the UK, you can look for the 'Grown in Britain' symbol, which means the product has been sustainably harvested. Not only will you reduce your carbon footprint, but you can achieve better results in your cookouts.

ADDING SEASONED WOOD CHUNKS

If you want to add bigger smoky flavours to your cookout, just add seasoned wood chunks.

A hot dynamic burning fire produces light smoky wood flavours; a lower burning fire will produce a heavier smoke with more acrid tars and acids. Think about when you stand over a slow-burning fire and your eyes sting from smoke – this is from unburnt fuel from a fire that is not hot enough. The most efficient fire will seem virtually smokeless because its smoke is the beautiful cleaner flavoured smoke that is better to cook with.

Putting wet wood or soaked wood chips into your coals takes energy away from the fire and produces a heavy smoke – this is a bad way of smoking and will not produce the food you want. Even putting dry wood into a fire that's not hot enough will do the same. If you want to use chips, wrap them in foil. That way they won't flare up. Don't soak them.

I normally add seasoned wood chunks to my coals once they start to glow. If I'm doing a long cook, I will add larger logs as they will last longer and I don't have to keep topping up the fuel (see p16 for more on this).

I like to use seasoned wood chunks from local sustainable woodlands. The best wood to use is the wood that's local. Stay away from wet woods or woods with resin, such as pine.

Seasoned wood basically means the wood has been dried – remember, a wet wood will take a lot of energy out of your cooker and you won't get a clean burn. Look for a moisture rating of 17.5–21%.

My favourite seasoned woods to cook with are sweet chestnut, wild cherry, birch, alder, ash, oak, plum, pear and beech - all of which are available in the UK.

The best way to source your wood is from your local woodsman or charcoal maker, though more garden centres and supermarkets are now stocking quality chunks of seasoned wood, as well as good lump wood charcoal all year round.

THE BEST SET-UP

Most people who are cooking BBQ in their backyards or at a park have a kettle-type grill with a lid. And this is how I cook the majority of my food. There are a couple of things to think about when building your heat source for your home cookout and getting the grill ready for cooking. So digest the information on this page, and then move on to the next pages to learn how to get your cooker rocking!

GET YOUR COOKER ROCKING

I learned to cook BBQ from my father, who learned to cook BBQ from his father.

My grandpa is from Bronson, Iowa and raised his four children in nearby Sioux City. He would load up the car with a cooker and enough food for an all-day feast, and then drive the family to a state park and just grill all day. Chicken, ribs, burgers, spuds, loose meats (an Iowa classic) and veggies would all be on offer. Grandpa was also a square dance caller, a great storyteller and brilliant showman. My father picked up loads of techniques from him, which he passed on to me. My father was a single dad raising two young kids – and I was hyper as heck, so it could not have been easy. He would hand me a platter of raw food and send me down to the grill at the bottom of the garden to cook dinner. In the early days, I'd return with a load of burnt food, then I got the hang of it. Practice makes perfect, and I had plenty of practice.

Nowadays, I travel the world to see how other chefs, artisans and pitmasters use live fire to cook their amazing food. I learn new tricks and tips every day, and the more people I meet, the more knowledgeable I become in the art of cooking over live fire.

SEASONING THE GRILL

The best way to season a new grill is to get a fire going – a solid heat (200°C/400°F). Then spray vegetable oil inside the lid and on the grill. Let the heat cook the oil in for at least an hour. And the best way to keep it seasoned? Cook on it!

CLEANING THE GRILL

Once you have a well seasoned grill, you can use a lemon, onion or some type of acid like vinegar to clean it. Cut a lemon in half and rub it on the grill. Easy.

HOW TO LIGHT YOUR CHARCOAL

The ultimate way to get your cooker going is with the help of a chimney starter – it's cheap, easy to buy and will revolutionize your cookouts. It is basically an open-ended cylinder with a wire grate inside that allows you to pre-cook your coals before they hit the cooker. If you're adding more fuel mid-cook, a chimney starter is a good way to maintain a consistent temperature (as you're adding cooked coals).

To get it going, start by placing the chimney starter on the grill (if you're getting top-up fuel ready, make sure the chimney starter is on a fireproof surface. I usually place it on bricks). Next, fill the hollow chamber with some good charcoal. Take two sheets of newspaper and scrunch them up and place underneath the chimney grate (you can use any natural lighter or kindling). Set fire to the paper, and once the top coals glow red, pour the whole lot into your cooker. Then lay them out in the way required for the technique specified for your recipe (see Set-Up Techniques on page 14).

This is a good time to add a couple of chunks of seasoned wood. You can also use fire bricks to help build a reservoir of heat. Place one or two next to the fire. If the fire gets too hot, the bricks will absorb some of the heat; they will also store heat and keep a cook more consistent.

If you don't have a chimney starter, the best way to build a fire is to use the teepee method. Place scrunched up newspaper, natural fire lighters or kindling in the middle of the base, build a circle of charcoal around it and get it flaming. When it gets going, add coals on top, building the teepee. Don't pack it too tight or prod it – leave gaps to allow oxygen to reach the fuel, and avoid disrupting the airflow. Once the teepee is glowing, add more coals.

CONTROLLING THE HEAT

Fire responds to airflow and more fuel. You can control the airflow with the cooker pinwheels (air vents) or by using the lid.

To increase the heat in the cooker, add more fuel (ideally pre-cooked charcoal from a chimney starter, see p11). And/or open the pinwheels to allow oxygen in.

To bring the heat down, suffocate the fire with less airflow. You can also reduce the intensity of the fire by spreading out your charcoal, which stops the lumps from heating each other up.

Test the temperature of your cooker. Some recipes will give you a temperature range – you can use the techniques above to achieve this. Test the temperature by placing a thermometer roughly where you'll be placing your food.

If your cookout starts to flare up, suffocate the fuel. Close the pinwheels to reduce the airflow. And/or place the lid onto the cooker.

Sometimes the fats can catch fire and cause some flare-ups. You can suffocate the fuel or you can just take the food away from the grill until you get things under control. It's best to avoid a fat fire. In the immortal words of Tyson Ho from Arrogant Swine in New York, 'First rule of whole hog cooking, don't set fire to your hog.'

MY FAMILY ALBUM, PAGE 10

Shucking corn with my dad – in style! **(1)**

Grandpa has a full grill rocking with four chickens, ribs, my grandma's meatloaf, spuds, BBQ sauce and corn. **(2)**

With my boys: Blue, 17; Noah, 13; Frasier, 11. **(3)**

Grandpa hitting the reverse button on the vacuum cleaner to get the coals fired up. **(4)**

If I wasn't outdoors on the grill, I was in the kitchen with my mom and grandma. **(5)**

 ESSENTIAL ITEMS FOR THE ULTIMATE COOKOUT

A good outdoor cooker with a lid

Chimney starter (see How to Light Your Charcoal, p11)

Good-quality lump wood charcoal (see Alchemy of Fire, p6)

Seasoned wood chunks (preferably local and sustainable – see p9)

Fire bricks (see How to Light Your Charcoal, p11)

Plancha (or griddle pan or frying pan) – used in specific recipes, like the mac and cheese pancakes on page 38!

Good set of metal tongs (two pairs to avoid cross-contamination of raw and cooked meat) – these are an extension of your hands

Chopping boards (again, two is best for raw and cooked meat)

Metal spatula and silicon brush

Temperature probe (to check your meat is safely cooked, and your grill is hot enough)

Herb wand – tie loads of bunches of herbs to a stick or a wooden spoon, then use this herb wand to brush meat with oils, butters and marinades

Cooler full of cold beer/cider

Buddies, music, laughter

SET-UP TECHNIQUES

These techniques work for a classic kettle BBQ or similar. If you don't have a base grill (like the pictures on the right), simply load the charcoal into the bottom of the cooker.

INDIRECT VS DIRECT HEAT

People tend to load the bottom of the cooker with charcoal without leaving an indirect zone. By this I mean a side of the cooker where there is no direct fuel heating the food above. By having a direct side with fuel, and an indirect side without fuel, you'll have more control over the heat your food is getting. Food will still cook on the indirect side, as there's always residual heat in the whole cooker.

HALF AND HALF (1)

I use this technique most of the time. It's quick and super easy to set up. Once you have your coals cooking, lay them out over half of the base of your cooker. So one half of the base has no coals. This gives you a medium-hot heat available over the coals and a large indirect zone that gets you out of trouble, but still allows the food to cook. I normally have the bottom and top pinwheels fully open with this method.

DIRTY

For dirty cooking, you need a nice solid bed of coals. It's really important to make sure that the coals are kept in a tight slab so they don't burn away too fast. Blow over the coals to dust away the ash just before you place anything on them – so you don't have to brush ash off your food later. You will find it harder to get a char on the food, as there is not enough space for the oxygen to

combust and create extra heat before it hits your food – you are just using the static heat from the actual coals.

SLAB

Cover the entire base of the cooker in an even bed of coals. Be careful not to add too many as you don't have an indirect zone, so there's no real place for goof-proof cooking.

LONELY ISLAND (2)

This technique is for slow and low cooking. I prefer to use my offset firebox cooker when going for the long haul (see p16), but if you don't have one, the lonely island technique will work too. Bear in mind it will require the fuel to be topped up every 50–70 minutes. And when you lift the lid, you lose the heat, so if you're looking, you ain't cooking! Place a small number of cooked coals on one side of the base in a small pile. Your joint of meat will need to be placed on the other side of the grill over indirect heat. I usually go with 8–12 chunks of lump wood charcoal, and then place a couple of wood chunks on top. For the best way to top up the fuel, see page 16.

TARGET (3)

This does what it says on the tin. Lay out your coals in an even circular pile right in the middle of the cooker, leaving the perimeter clear of coals just like a target bullseye on a dart board. This is a great technique when grilling burgers and toasting buns – you can char them on the direct heat, and then move them to the perimeter so they continue

cooking on the indirect heat without burning. It gives you a chance to get another round of food cooking.

HEAT CANYON (4)

If you own a Weber-style kettle grill BBQ, they normally come with metal boxes or separators to help hold the coals to the side. Once you have your coals cooking, the cooked coals need to be placed on the opposite sides of the base of your cooker, allowing just enough room in the middle of the cooker for a drip pan. This technique is great for big joints of meat, whole fish and large vegetables. By putting the lid on top, you turn your outdoor grill into an outdoor oven. Playing with the pinwheels will help you to control your temperature. Suffocate the airflow to lower the temperature.

RING OF FIRE (5)

This is another excellent way to cook your food using indirect heat. Place the coals in a ring toward the edge of the cooker. This provides an even cook for large cuts of meat and big veggies that need a long cook. This technique works just like the heat canyon.

OFFSET FIREBOX / PROPER SMOKER

This is a style of cooker, rather than a technique. It's great for cooking slow and low. The offset firebox has two chambers – one for cooking, one for fuel – which means you can keep topping up the fuel without letting the heat out of the main chamber. We use this type of cooker on the festival circuit when we cook pork shoulder and brisket slow and low. Using an offset firebox always takes a bit of extra prep time, but is worth it if you're serious about slow and low cooking. It's a good idea to invest in a smoker that is designed for long cooks. You can still achieve great results on the classic kettle, but it's just not as easy to control the heat for the long haul.

TOPPING — UP FUEL — MID-COOK

Most of the recipes in the All Day & All of the Night chapter (slow and low!) will require you to top up the fuel mid-cook. If you're using a kettle-type cooker (rather than an offset or proper smoker) you'll need to remember these top tips!

- Add fuel every 50–70 minutes.

- Add a large handful of uncooked lump wood charcoal – about 8–10 coals is ideal. You can use the chimney starter to pre-cook the coals and maintain a constant heat in your cooker, but it's not essential.

- However! If you're using charcoal briquettes, you have to pre-cook them before topping up as the chemical binder used to make them can taint the taste of your food.

TOP TIPS

1 IF YOU'RE USING CHARCOAL BRIQUETTES, USE WISELY.

I wouldn't advise using briquettes, but if you have a bunch of mates on their way over, and nothing else to hand, remember this: make sure they go grey before you put any food on the grill. Some briquettes use chemical binders that can taint the taste of food. For the same reason, don't add this kind of charcoal to a BBQ mid-cook unless the briquettes are grey. But you can add cold lump wood charcoal to your cooker without tainting the taste of the meat.

2 UNDERSTAND THE ASH BED.

An ash bed can suffocate your fuel, but not in all cases! Charcoal briquettes do not like an ash bed, while lump wood charcoal benefits from a small ash bed. And you might want to use an ash bed to help you control your heat, bringing the temperature down — when you're cooking fish, for example.

3 MAKE SURE YOUR MEAT IS AT ROOM TEMPERATURE.

That thing is a muscle. It needs to relax. Don't make it angry by taking it from the fridge and throwing it straight on the heat.

It won't like it and you can do better. Pull it out of the fridge 30 minutes to an hour before cooking, depending on the size.

4 DON'T CUT INTO YOUR MEAT TO SEE IF IT'S DONE.

Poke your red meat. If it's squishy, it'll be on the rare side. If it bounces back, it's more on the well-done side. For more tips on cooking the perfect steak, head to the Perfect Steak recipe (p100).

5 USE A TEMPERATURE PROBE.

A meat thermometer will help you be sure your food is cooked and safe to eat. Insert the probe into the thickest part of the meat and follow the temperature guides in the recipes.

6 REST YOUR MEAT.

Don't spoil the fruits of your hard grilling/smoking/roasting labour — rest that meat! It allows the steak/joint to stay nice and juicy. Everyone rests a chicken, but they cut straight into a grilled steak. Wrong! That meat needs resting too. Rest it for about half the time you cooked it. And the bigger your joint, the longer you should let it chill on a board.

BREAKFAST HEROES & AFTERNOON DELIGHTS

GET YOUR WHOLE DAY ROCKING — FROM
MORNING TACOS TO MIGHTY AFTERNOON SUBS

FRENCH TOAST GRILLED CHEESE

A couple of years ago, while having French toast in a French restaurant in New York City, I had the epiphany: French toast is great for breakfast, but it actually works at any time of the day, especially 2am when you have the munchies.

 SERVES 2

🍖 **BBQ SET-UP**
   Slab technique

6 rashers (slices) of dry cured smoked streaky bacon

4 eggs

Couple of pinches of cayenne pepper

4 slices of white bread

50g (1¾oz) butter, plus extra if needed

150g (5½oz) mature Cheddar cheese, grated (shredded)

Maple syrup, for drizzling

Get a large cast-iron frying pan (skillet) heated up on the grill. Chuck all your bacon straight into the hot pan and fry until crispy, turning once, then leave to drain on kitchen (paper) towel. Wipe out the frying pan with kitchen towel and leave on the heat.

While the bacon is frying, whisk the eggs in a wide bowl with the cayenne pepper. Pour the egg mixture into a tray that is just big enough for four slices of bread. Place the bread in the egg mixture and let it soak in, turn the slices and soak again. Melt the butter in the hot pan and fry each soaked slice of bread on one side until golden. Place two of the cooked slices golden side up on a board. Layer the cheese and bacon on top of the bread, top with the remaining slices golden side down.

Finish these titans of breakfast in the hot pan, adding a little more butter if needed. They will need about 1–2 minutes on each side until the cheese is melted and the bread is golden all over.

Rest the sandwiches on a board for a minute, cut in half and serve with maple syrup drizzled all over.

You have just made the best breakfast that has ever existed. Your friends, family and random strangers will praise you and your cooking prowess. Now go forth and prosper.

BREAKFAST TACOS

These tacos are great for a late breakfast, lunch or any time of day. I usually make breakfast tacos every other week. The kids love them and my hungover mates swear by their medicinal properties for healing their souls.

🍴 **SERVES 4**

🪑 **BBQ SET-UP**
Half and half technique

1 red (bell) pepper

1 green (bell) pepper

2 red chillies

1 green chilli

200g (7oz) chorizo, sliced and diced

6 eggs

50ml (1¾ fl oz/scant ¼ cup) whole milk

Black pepper

For the pickled radish

100ml (3½fl oz/scant ½ cup) red wine vinegar

2 tbsp light brown sugar

6 radishes, thinly sliced

For the pico de gallo

2 beef tomatoes, chopped

1 red onion, chopped

Bunch of coriander (cilantro), chopped

Juice of 2 limes

Sea salt

To serve

12 corn or flour tortillas (or both) 200g (7oz) Cheddar cheese, grated (shredded)

1 avocado, mashed

First, cut your peppers in half, deseed them, then get the pepper halves and chillies on the grill over a direct heat and roast for about 30 minutes with the lid on.

While they're roasting, make a quick pickle. Mix the vinegar and sugar in a bowl until the sugar dissolves. Throw in the radishes and leave to pickle for 15 minutes.

Now is a good time to make your fresh pico de gallo salsa. Add all the ingredients to a bowl, mix and season with salt. If you like, you could make a huge batch and save for an afternoon snack with tortilla chips.

When the peppers and chillies are ready, remove from the heat and set aside to cool. Roughly chop and set aside.

Place a frying pan (skillet) over the direct side to get some heat into it. Add the chorizo and fry until crispy and releasing all the natural oils. Whisk the eggs and milk together, season with a pinch of pepper and add to the chorizo. Now add the peppers and chillies. Lightly fold through the egg mixture and pull the pan off the grill (or onto the indirect side) so the eggs don't dry out. The eggs cook super-quick so be ready. Don't fiddle with your junk! People are hungry – heck, you are hungry!

Quickly toast your tortillas on the grill. I sometimes flick a bit of water onto them to stop them drying out. Pull them off, then build your tacos. Start with the cheese on the bottom to help it melt, then add the scrambled egg concoction. Next top with the avocado, pico de gallo and the pickled radish and eat. Fuel that body! Get ready to start your day off righteously.

KOREAN PHILLY CHEESE STEAK

I came up with this recipe over a year ago when I was approached by a video game company to create a classic Philadelphia staple, but with a Korean twist. I did my research and worked on a bulgogi marinade for the meat and mushrooms. The video game is set in Philadelphia in 2020, when the city is occupied by the North Korean People's Army. In our YouTube video, I play an insurgent fighting for freedom. Sounds far fetched? Check it out – we spent $500 on after-affects. Whoooohooooo! Marinate the meat overnight for optimum flavour and meat tenderness.

🍴 **SERVES 4**

🍖 **BBQ SET-UP**
Half and half technique

1.5kg (3lb 5oz) sirloin steak or flank or skirt

1 onion, peeled and halved

6–8 large mushrooms

For the bulgogi marinade

1 Asian pear, peeled and chopped

1 red onion, chopped

3 garlic cloves, chopped

2 smoked garlic cloves (optional, see p70)

2.5cm (1 inch) ginger, chopped

2 tbsp soy sauce

1 tbsp sesame oil

1 tsp chilli flakes (if you can get a hold of isot pul biber flakes, use them – they are amazing)

1 tbsp honey

1 tbsp brown sugar

2 spring onions (scallions), chopped

Put the steak into a freezer bag and place in the freezer for a couple of hours. This will enable you to slice the meat extra thin.

When it's ready, use a very sharp knife to slice the steak across the grain lengthways into 2mm (¹⁄₁₆-inch) strips.

Add all the marinade ingredients, apart from the spring onions to a blender and pulse. Or use a stick blender. Once blended, add in the spring onions.

Place the sliced meat and the marinade into a ziplock bag and leave to marinate overnight or at least for a couple hours.

Get your coals cooking and prepare to cook. Place the halved onion onto the grill over the direct heat.

Remove the meat from the marinade, reserving the leftover sauce for the mushrooms. Throw the mushrooms and marinade into a bowl and mix it up so that the boomers can absorb the lovely flavours. Cook the mushrooms alongside the onion for 6–8 minutes until tender and juicy.

Recipe continues...

To serve

Olive oil

4 sub rolls, halved

250g (9oz/2 cups) grated
(shredded) cheese

50g (1¾oz/⅓ cup) sesame
seeds, toasted

Recipe continued from p25

Now it's beef time. Using a pair of tongs, lay out each strip of
beef over the direct heat for a quick grill. This will take 30–45
seconds a side depending on the thickness of the steak and
the temperature of your grill.

You basically want to get a good char happening on the
meat, and the sugar will help that, but remember, sugar
burns – so keep an eye on your steak strips.

Take all the cooked food off the grill. Roughly chop up the
mushrooms and onions. Drizzle a little olive oil onto the cut
side of your meat roll and toast on the grill.

Now it's time to assemble this beast of a cheese steak
sandwich. I like to hit the sub twice with cheese. One layer
straight on the hot toasted bread, then a big old handful of
steak, onions, mushrooms, then more cheese. Finish off with
the sesame seeds and condiment – I like mayo or mustard.
Then enjoy your tasty cheese steak sandwich.

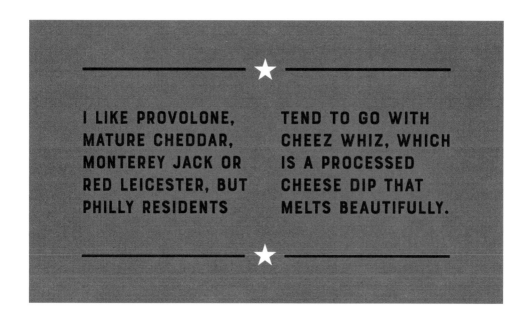

I LIKE PROVOLONE, MATURE CHEDDAR, MONTEREY JACK OR RED LEICESTER, BUT PHILLY RESIDENTS TEND TO GO WITH CHEEZ WHIZ, WHICH IS A PROCESSED CHEESE DIP THAT MELTS BEAUTIFULLY.

CRAB CAKE SANDWICH WITH AVOCADO AND CORN SALSA

★ ★

'Maryland is for Crabs'. That was my state motto growing up. Our neighbouring state, Virginia, had a much better motto, 'Virginia is for Lovers'. Way sexier than ours. As a small child, we would go crabbing all the time. I would tie some string around some chicken necks and lower them into the water by the docks near my grandma's house. Then in 1989/90, I worked in an all-you-can-eat crab house called A.T. Lantic's Seafood House. The owner came up with the name because he wanted it to appear first in the phonebook under 'seafood restaurants'. The chef, Dan Sacharoff, made the best crab cakes ever! I've tried them all over the eastern seaboard and Dan's couldn't be topped – until now! Let's get to it.

🍴 **SERVES 4**

🍖 **BBQ SET-UP**
Target technique

For the crab cakes

4 spring onions (scallions), finely chopped

1 red or green chilli, finely chopped

Zest of 1 lemon

2 tbsp mayonnaise

2 tbsp plain yoghurt

1 tbsp yellow mustard

1 tsp Old Bay American seafood seasoning, or any seafood seasoning

Drizzle of Tabasco sauce

Drizzle of Worcestershire sauce

1 egg white

2 slices of day-old bread, finely chopped, or breadcrumbs

In a large bowl, mix together all the ingredients for the crab cakes, except the crabmeat. Make sure it is well mixed, then carefully fold in the crab. You need to make sure you don't break up the meat too much. Season with salt and pepper. Divide the mixture into four balls and shape them into patties. Rest them on non-stick paper in the fridge for at least 30 minutes.

Meanwhile, make the salsa. You can grill your corn cobs over in the husks or wihout – you get a nice char on the kernals if you do it without. Grill over the direct heat for 6–8 minutes, turning regularly. Move to the indirect side if the corn goes too brown. Take the cobs off the grill, stand them vertically and slice the kernels off. Then, mix all the salsa ingredients together in a bowl, season to taste, and set aside.

Get a cast-iron frying pan (skillet) on the direct heat and get that baby hot (the target technique basically turns the cooker into a stovetop). Add in the oil, and when it's hot, carefully fry the crab cakes for about 4–5 minutes on the first side, until you have a brown crust.

Recipe continues...

450g (1lb) fresh white
  crabmeat

100g (3½oz) fresh brown
  crabmeat

1 tbsp olive oil, for frying

Sea salt and black pepper

For the salsa

2 corn on the cobs

1 avocado, flesh diced

1 mango, flesh diced

½ red onion, chopped

1 red chilli, chopped

Juice of 1 lime

Bunch of flat-leaf parsley,
  chopped

Sea salt and black pepper

To serve

4 brioche buns

4 lettuce leaves

1 lemon, cut into wedges

Recipe continued from p28

Using a fish slice, carefully turn the crab cakes and fry for another 4–5 minutes on the other side.

Remove and rest on kitchen (paper) towel for 5 minutes. Meanwhile, toast the brioche buns. You can use the direct heat over the target to get a nice char, and then move to the indirect side to keep warm.

Assemble the crab cake sandwiches by layering the bun base with lettuce, then a crab cake, then a large dollop of salsa. Follow with the top of the bun and skewer a lemon wedge on the top. Ooooooh yeeeeaah! Dig in!! The state of Maryland will be proud.

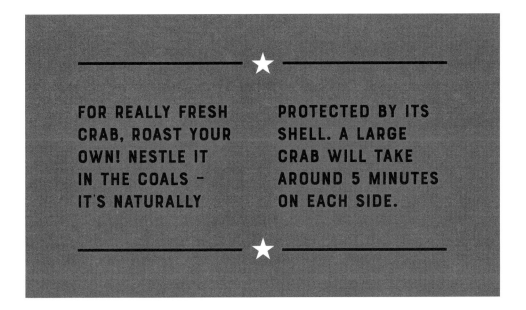

FOR REALLY FRESH CRAB, ROAST YOUR OWN! NESTLE IT IN THE COALS – IT'S NATURALLY PROTECTED BY ITS SHELL. A LARGE CRAB WILL TAKE AROUND 5 MINUTES ON EACH SIDE.

SPICY MACKEREL MELT

My kids love a tuna melt and this is a spin on that classic recipe. Mackerel is a really healthy fish with lots of essential oils, plus it has a great texture and just loves live fire. Fish can sometimes be daunting to cook on a grill, but this is a fool-proof recipe that kids, adults and even dogs love. Plus, it's got cheese in it, which is always good. I usually use a freshly sliced sourdough loaf for that awesome crunch! If you can't get hold of one, a sliced loaf, baguette or paninis will be just as good.

✎ **SERVES 4**

🍴 **BBQ SET-UP**
Half and half technique. Seasoned wood chunks

2 large mackerel, gutted

4 slices sourdough bread

A bunch of spring onions (scallions), roughly chopped, plus a few extra, sliced, to garnish

2 heaped tsp mayonnaise

100g (3½oz) mature Cheddar cheese, grated (shredded)

Sea salt and black pepper

1 red chilli, sliced, to garnish

Thoroughly dry the mackerel skins with kitchen (paper) towel. Lightly score the skin and season with salt and pepper. Gently place the fish on the grill over the direct heat. You are looking for a medium heat. After a couple of minutes, carefully turn the mackerel over, using a fish slice. After another couple of minutes, move the fish to the indirect side and cover with the lid for another 2–4 minutes, until just cooked through. Remove and set aside to rest for 5 minutes.

Lightly toast one side of the sourdough slices on the grill and set aside. Once the fish has rested, remove the skin and flake the flesh into a large bowl, being very careful to remove the bones as you go. Gently fold in the spring onions and mayo. Season with salt and pepper and spread on the toasted side of each slice of sourdough.

Sprinkle the cheese over the top and place on the indirect side of the grill, with the lid on, until the cheese is melted. If you have a cloche, use that to cover the food for a quicker melt. You can easily cheat the melt by using a blow torch.

Garnish with the extra spring onion slices and chillies and enjoy your awesomeness. You just made a tasty dish that the kids will go apeshit for.

LAMB KEEMADILLA

India meats Mexico... get it? ... meats? oh... ok.

🍴 **SERVES 4**

🍸 **BBQ SET-UP**
   Half and half technique

1 tbsp cumin seeds

2 tbsp coriander seeds

10 peppercorns

10 whole cloves

30g (1oz/2 tbsp) butter

2 red onions, chopped

1 tsp mustard seeds

2 star anise

1 cinnamon stick

6 garlic cloves, finely
   chopped

5cm (2 inches) ginger,
   peeled and finely
   chopped

1 red chilli, sliced

1 tsp ground turmeric

1 x 400g (14oz) can
   chopped tomatoes

500g (1lb 2oz) lamb
   mince (ground lamb)

200g (7oz/1⅓ cups) frozen
   peas

1 tbsp garam masala

8 flour tortilla wraps

300g (10½oz) mature
   Cheddar cheese, grated
   (shredded)

Handful of coriander
   (cilantro) leaves

First, dry-fry the cumin, coriander, peppercorns and cloves in a large cast-iron frying pan (skillet) over the direct heat for 2–3 minutes until fragrant. Careful they don't burn. Tip them into a pestle and mortar and crush to a fine powder. In India, this is called a dhania jeera powder and is an amazing foundation on which to build your palace of aromatic king-like flavours.

Place the same pan back on the direct heat. Add the butter. When melted, add the red onion, mustard seeds, star anise and cinnamon stick. Fry these suckers for at least 15–20 minutes until the onions are caramelized – you can add a little water if they start to catch. Chuck in the garlic, ginger, chilli, turmeric, dhania jeera and tomatoes. Cook for another 5–10 minutes until the sauce is reduced and awesome.

Now it's time for meat! Move all your keema sauce to one side of the pan. Add the lamb mince to the empty side. Fry the meat until it is brown and crispy, then mix it with the sauce and cook together for about 30–40 minutes until most of the moisture has evaporated. Add in the peas, along with the garam masala, and cook for a further 5 minutes.

Transfer the keema from the pan to a bowl. (It can be frozen once cool or kept in the fridge for 3–4 days for your next helping – I find that the keema tastes better after a couple of days in the fridge anyway, so the flavours can fuse.)

Wipe out your pan and get it back on the heat. Lay four of the tortilla wraps on a board and spread a good layer of the keema filling on each one. Sprinkle each one with a quarter of the cheese and top with one of the other four wraps. Using a large spatula, place a keemadilla in the hot pan and toast for a minute or so. Lightly press down with the spatula to make sure the cheese melts and holds everything together. It's good to move the pan between the direct and indirect heat to ensure you don't burn the keemadilla. Flip and brown the other side. Slide out onto a board, cut into pieces and top with coriander.

These go awesome with a cold lager and some classic heavy metal. Try Iron Maiden or Judas Priest. They can be a bit cheesy, which works well. I've put on Michael Bolton's greatest hits while cooking this dish and, I gotta admit, it tasted better.

SMOKY, TANGY, CHEESY MEATBALLY SUB SANDWICH FROM SMOKYCHEESEBALLVILLE

Back in my college days, our crew would hit up the local Italian joint called Ratsies. My go-to subs were the chicken parmigiana sub and this baby. I love meatballs, especially ones with a melted cheese nucleus.

🥄 **SERVES 4**

🍖 **BBQ SET-UP**
Heat canyon technique. Seasoned wood chunks

For the marinara sauce

4 tbsp olive oil

4 smoked garlic cloves, chopped (see p70)

2 tbsp capers, drained and roughly chopped

4 canned anchovy fillets, chopped

2 x 400g (14oz) cans chopped tomatoes

1 tsp dried oregano

For the meatballs

375g (13oz) beef mince (ground beef)

375g (13oz) pork mince (ground pork)

3 smoked garlic cloves, finely chopped (see p70)

1 tbsp dried basil

2 tsp black pepper

2 tsp sea salt

125g (4½oz) mozzarella

125g (4½oz) Gruyère cheese

4 sub rolls, to serve

Get your marinara sauce cooking, so it has time to do its thing. Place a medium saucepan on the direct side and pour in the olive oil. When it's hot, add the garlic, capers and anchovies. Fry for 2 minutes, then add the tomatoes and oregano. Leave to slowly simmer on the indirect side while you prep your other ingredients. You might want to add a bit of water if the sauce gets too thick.

Now, let's make meatballs. Place all your mince in a large bowl, along with the garlic, basil, pepper and salt. Mix well, so all the seasoning can work its way through all the mince. Divide and shape into eight balls. Grate your cheeses, mix together and put half to one side for the sub topping. Then use your thumb to make a hole in each meatball. Stuff loads of cheese inside. Manoeuvre the meat to cover over the cheese, or you can also keep a bit of mince on the side to plug the whole. Whichever technique works best for you.

Get your cooker to 180°C (350°F) – see page 12 for help with this. Throw in the seasoned wood chunks. Place the meatballs over the heat canyon on the indirect heat, and cook for 15–20 minutes until cooked through and you have a nice crust on the outside. These are done when they are done. They might even take 30 minutes or more.

Slice open and toast your rolls and get ready to assemble. I like to slice the meatballs in half and place them inside the roll, so the hot cheese doesn't ooze out and burn my mouth. Then smother with the hot marinara sauce and sprinkle more cheese on top. Nice work, people! How good is that meatball sub sandwich? 'Beyond good' is the correct answer.

MAC AND CHEESE PANCAKE WITH MOJO ROJO SAUCE

★ ★

My kids love their mac and cheese. Of course, they always want the toxic orange stuff that comes in the box. That was the case until I started making this recipe for them. The mojo rojo sauce was inspired by Spanish chef Nieves Barragán Mohacho – we collaborated on a burger to raise money for Action Against Hunger. I did a twice-smoked aioli for the bun base and Nieves added her mojo rojo. This is my version of said sauce!

🍳 **SERVES 4**

🍖 **BBQ SET-UP**
   Half and half technique

For the mojo rojo sauce

4 Romano peppers, deseeded and roughly chopped

8 garlic cloves, roughly chopped

3 jalapeño chillies, deseeded and roughly chopped

1 tbsp cumin seeds, toasted and crushed

2 tbsp smoked paprika

Handful of coriander (cilantro) leaves

Handful of thyme leaves

2 rehydrated chipotle chillies

3 tbsp balsamic vinegar

3 tbsp extra virgin olive oil

2 tsp salt

First, make the mojo rojo sauce. In a food processor, blitz all the ingredients up to and including the chipotle chillies. Once blended, pour into a bowl and stir in the vinegar, oil and salt. Boomtown! You just made one banging sauce.

Now make a next-level mac and cheese. You can do this bit on the outdoor cooker, but it's a bit easier in the kitchen. First, boil the pasta until al dente and drain. Set aside.

In a medium saucepan, whisk the butter, flour and milk over a medium heat until smooth and thick. You are making a quick white sauce. Once the sauce is bubbling and the flour is cooked out, add all the cheese, the mustard and the jalapeño slices. Keep stirring until melted and awesome.

Throw the cooked pasta into the cheese sauce, stir well and leave to cool for an hour or so. This recipe works better when the mac and cheese is cold. I'm a firm believer that mac and cheese tastes better the next day.

When you are ready to eat, get your outdoor cooker going. Divide the cooled mac and cheese into eight balls of awesomeness. On the direct side melt the extra 2 tablespoons of butter in a frying pan (skillet). Throw a couple of the mac and cheese balls into the pan and use your spatula to flatten them into pancakes.

Recipe continues...

For the macaroni

350g (12oz) macaroni pasta tubes

50g (1¾oz) butter, plus 2 tbsp for frying

50g (1¾oz) plain (all-purpose) flour

400ml (14fl oz/1⅔ cups) whole milk

300g (10½oz) red Leicester cheese, grated (shredded)

100g (3½oz) Roquefort or blue cheese

2 tbsp Dijon mustard

1 jalapeño chilli, sliced

Handful of coriander (cilantro) leaves, chopped, to garnish

Recipe continued from p38

Fry the pancakes until you have a thick golden crust. Then flip and fry the other side.

You might lose a couple of stray bits of macaroni when you flip, but don't fret, just let them crisp up. They are actually part of the recipe – you are going to top everything with these mac and cheese 'burnt ends'.

When you have a thick crust on both sides, remove the pancakes from the heat and repeat with the remaining ones. When they are all cooked, spoon the mojo rojo sauce over the pancakes and top with the chopped coriander. Throw those burnt ends on top and astound your friends with your amazing cooking skills and garlic breath. (Don't try to suck face later, or make sure your partner has some too!)

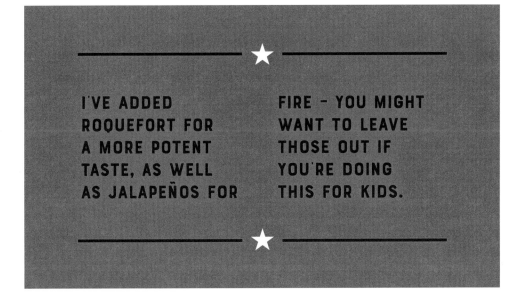

I'VE ADDED ROQUEFORT FOR A MORE POTENT TASTE, AS WELL AS JALAPEÑOS FOR FIRE - YOU MIGHT WANT TO LEAVE THOSE OUT IF YOU'RE DOING THIS FOR KIDS.

ALL DAY & ALL OF THE NIGHT

THESE RECIPES CAN TAKE MOST OF THE DAY TO COOK – SLOW AND LOW, BABY! – BUT BEST THINGS COME TO THOSE WHO WAIT

THE PERFECT BUTT
- PULLED PORK

★ ★

Over the past six years, we've slow-cooked over 2,000 pork shoulders on the festival circuit. We've played with various cooking techniques and flavourings, and the recipe that we've unleashed in this book is the best way to achieve a delicious and tender pulled pork sandwich. People often say we make the best pulled pork they've ever tasted. Well, my friends, we've done some major developing and put in some super-long hours to bring you the ultimate pulled pork recipe in the history of the planet.

🍴 SERVES 12

🍖 BBQ SET-UP

Offset firebox or proper smoker (or lonely island technique). For the lonely island technique, I use a mix of charcoal and seasoned fruit wood chunks. On the smoker, I tend to use more wood, starting with a fruit wood/charcoal mix and switching over to hard woods like oak and sweet chestnut. Mixing charcoal with the wood helps to keep a consistent heat

Get your cooker to 110ºC (235ºF). Temperatures can fluctuate and you are in this for the long haul, so make sure you are always rocking at between 107 and 120ºC (225–250ºF). I'm always happy if I am within this range. For more help on this, see Controlling the Heat on page 12.

It is a balancing act between keeping the right temperature and getting the right smoke. You want to see a clean white smoke coming out of your chimney. You don't want to see it bellowing out. It will do this in the beginning, especially if you are using loads of wood, but as it breaks down and turns into charcoal, the white smoke shouldn't be as thick and fast and furious.

Let your pork joint get to room temperature. While this is happening, mix together the rub ingredients in a large bowl. When the meat is ready, liberally rub the pork with the spice mix, then place the joint in your smoker or onto your grill on the indirect heat. If you are using a kettle type cooker, make sure the joint is over the drip pan. Put the lid on.

Once you put the joint on the grill, don't look at it for at least 2–3 hours! Every time you look at it, you let all the heat out and this can cause 'meat stall', where the connective tissues don't have a chance to break down properly.

Recipe continues...

1 pork shoulder (butt) (around 4kg/9lb), neck bone and rind removed, chine bone removed, blade bone in, with a thin layer of fat, at room temperature

For the rub

1 tbsp dark brown sugar

1 tbsp sea salt

1 tbsp black pepper

1 tbsp onion granules

1 tbsp garlic granules

1 tbsp paprika

For the baste

240ml (8fl oz/1 cup) apple juice

240ml (8fl oz/1 cup) cider vinegar

1 tbsp chilli flakes (optional)

Recipe continued from p44

You do need to keep an eye on the temperature and the smoke though, and keep your fuel topped up. Go to page 16 for advice on adding fuel.

While the pork is roasting, make your baste sauce by combining the ingredients in a bowl. Grab a ladle and get ready for dousing.

Once the pork joint takes on a dark mahogany colour and there's a nice crack in the fat, it's time to pull it out for the next phase. Don't worry if there's some black bits on the outside – this is called the bark and it's all part of the slow and low cooking process.

Lay out a 1m-long (3ft) sheet of foil, then on top lay out a cross made from two 1m-long (3ft) sheets of butcher (peach) paper. Place the pork onto the butcher paper and douse it with ladlefuls of baste mix. You'll need to work quickly and create a slight bowl with the paper to keep the liquid in. Wrap the paper around the pork in layers, flipping the joint after each layer. Make sure the layers are not too tight – you need some airflow around the joint so that the baste sauce can infuse into the meat and help to keep it moist and sweet.

Put the wrapped pork back into the cooker and keep it going for another 5 hours at the same temperature. The slower and lower the better. I find that pulled pork cooked for 10 hours tastes good, 12 hours tastes better, 14 hours is next-level and 16 hours is what I call 'butter'. It all depends on how much time you have and how hungry you are. Our 5kg (11lb) festival pork shoulders get a minimum of 21 hours of slow and low smoky love.

Take the pork off and use tongs or forks to break the meat apart and pull it. If you hit this thing right, the blade bone should come out clean. Sing out 'clean bone!' and show it off to your friends and family. When pulling, try and keep some big chunks together. If you shred it too much, the meat can dry out. Make sure you mix that bark into the internal meat as it's had the seasoning and oxidization.

JAPANESE PORK BELLY

A combination of bacon and pork scratchings – two of the best inventions ever. If this dish were a song, it would be a floor filler. You can't not dance to pork belly. Pork belly can be a challenge to cook, as you need to render down the layers of fat. But I'm here to guide you through, and high-five you when you've nailed it.

✎ **SERVES 6-8**

🍖 **BBQ SET-UP**
   Half and half technique

1.2kg (2lb 10oz) pork belly, rind removed, fat scored

Tortilla wraps, to serve

4 spring onions (scallions), sliced, to serve

For the rub

1 tbsp sea salt

2 tsp ground ginger

1 tsp chilli flakes

2 tsp black pepper

For the glaze

100ml (3½fl oz/scant ½ cup) Japanese soy sauce

200ml (7fl oz/generous ¾ cup) mirin

2 tbsp white miso paste

100ml (3½fl oz/scant ½ cup) Japanese rice vinegar

1 tbsp sesame oil

1 tbsp honey

Get your cooker stupidly hot. Like a furnace from hell. We are talking 250–275ºC (480–530ºF).

Mix the rub ingredients together in a bowl. Mix the glaze ingredients together in a separate bowl. This is a fresh glaze so you don't need to cook it. Measure 100ml (3½fl oz/scant ½ cup) of the glaze into the spice mix. Make sure you've scored the fat on the pork belly, and rub the mix all over the belly.

Place the wet rubbed pork belly fat side up on the indirect side of the grill and get the lid on. After about 15–20 minutes, the glaze will start to char and you need to slow the cook down. Here's where we challenge your fire management skills. You need to drop the heat down and get your cooker to 115–130ºC (240–270ºF). To do this, suffocate your fuel and cut off the oxygen flow by closing the pinwheels (vents) on the cooker. For more help on this, see Controlling the Heat on page 12.

Once your cooker is stable, leave the pork belly to cook. Brush the glaze on every 45 minutes. Keep the lid down and only look when glazing or topping up fuel. Remember, if you're looking, it ain't cooking. Go to page 16 for advice on adding fuel.

Timing depends on the animal, your cooker – basically, it's done when it's done. I've cooked this recipe in 2½ hours and I've also taken 6 hours. So, how do you tell when it's done? Well, pork belly needs to be tender, but not falling apart. You want a little bit of a bite. But you need to get those fats to render down for flavour. You don't want to chew through lukewarm fat. You'll know when it's done by the 'meat wobble' – it should jiggle like jelly to the touch. You can also use a spoon to press into the fat. When there's a good amount of give, then you are ready to feast. If it's still tough and unforgiving, you need to keep going. Once done, leave to rest for 20 minutes.

Then slice into slabs of tasty porkalicious goodness! Pop onto a tortilla and sprinkle with spring onions.

BBQ SPAG BOL

Spag bol (ragu) is pretty much a staple dish in most homes, and is best cooked slow and low. This winter, my mate T-Bone and I started experimenting and developing a BBQ version in the cold and wet UK. You are welcome, because it is so ding dong dang delicious. It does take a bit of time, but is just as impressive as the 6-hour curry your mate Larry is always bragging about. Most spag bol recipes use beef mince (ground beef), but this one starts with a big ol' hunk of chuck (shoulder). The fattier the cut, the better. Good fat is good flavour.

✎ **SERVES 6**

🍴 **BBQ SET-UP: JOINT**
Offset firebox or proper smoker (or lonely island technique). Oak or nut smoking wood chunks

🍴 **BBQ SET-UP: SAUCE**
Half and half technique

3 large dirty onions
  (see p134)

1 smoked garlic bulb
  (see p70)

1kg (2lb 4oz) joint of chuck
  (beef shoulder), at room
  temperature

Sea salt and black pepper

450g (1lb) spaghetti

100g (3½oz) Parmesan
  cheese, shaved, to serve

Large bunch of rocket
  (arugula), to serve

Get your onions and garlic bulb cooking. The onions and garlic will slow-cook while the beef does its thing. For more instructions, see Dirty Onions p134, and Smoked Garlic p70).

Speaking of the beef, you need to season it. Rub it all over with salt and pepper, and place it as far from the coals as you can, on the indirect side of the BBQ (or in the offset firebox). Throw some seasoned wood chunks onto the coals and close the lid. Maintain the temperature of 150°C (300°F) all the way through and keep the fuel topped up. For more help on this, see Controlling the Heat on page 12. Go to page 16 for advice on adding fuel.

After an hour, check to see if the garlic and onions are tender. If they are, pull them off to rest, if not, spin them and cook for another 30 minutes. Spin and flip the beef joint, so all sides get a good hit of slow, low love. After 3–4 hours, the meat will be getting tender. When it's tender, take the joint off the BBQ and let it rest for 30 minutes.

Rebuild your fire to a medium heat, adding more coals to create the half and half technique. Once the meat has rested, finely chop the beef using a sharp knife. You are essentially making a beef mince with the smoked chuck joint. Set aside, then peel and finely chop both the garlic cloves and onion.

Heat a large saucepan over the direct heat and add the oil. Once the oil is hot, add the beef, garlic and onion. Fry for a couple of minutes, then add the wine. Boil for 2–3 minutes.

Recipe continues...

For the sauce

2 tbsp olive oil

250ml (9fl oz/generous 1 cup) red wine

4 x 400g (14oz) cans chopped tomatoes

3 tbsp tomato paste

2 tbsp dried rosemary

2 tbsp dried oregano

1 tbsp cider vinegar

1 tbsp balsamic vinegar

Recipe continued from p51

Add the rest of the ingredients for the sauce and season. Move the pan further towards the indirect side, so you can now slowly cook the sauce for about 45–60 minutes. You can go longer and slower – it will only get better. You might need to add a little water if it starts to dry out and reduce.

Once your sauce is rich and smoky, season to taste. Then get your pasta cooked in the kitchen. You are now ready to chow down on a next-level spag bol! Plate up and top with Parmesan shavings and rocket. Nice work, people.

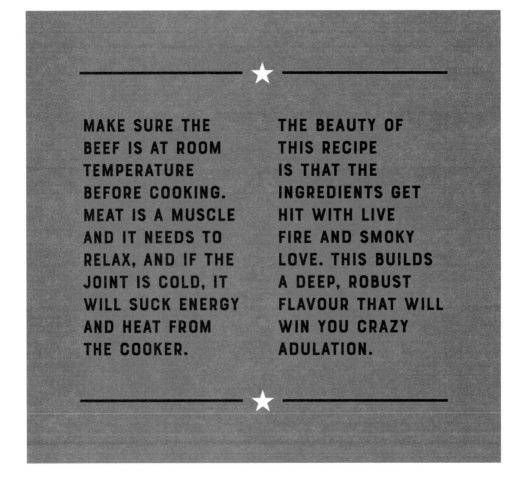

MAKE SURE THE BEEF IS AT ROOM TEMPERATURE BEFORE COOKING. MEAT IS A MUSCLE AND IT NEEDS TO RELAX, AND IF THE JOINT IS COLD, IT WILL SUCK ENERGY AND HEAT FROM THE COOKER.

THE BEAUTY OF THIS RECIPE IS THAT THE INGREDIENTS GET HIT WITH LIVE FIRE AND SMOKY LOVE. THIS BUILDS A DEEP, ROBUST FLAVOUR THAT WILL WIN YOU CRAZY ADULATION.

NEXT-LEVEL LAMB WRAP

★ ★

I love lamb almost as much as I love lamp. Sorry, *Anchorman* joke. Lamb is easily one of my favourite meats to cook and lamb fat is the best. There is no better flavour in my opinion. It's quite common to cook a leg of lamb or shoulder in the oven. But how about smoking one of these working muscles? The shoulder has loads of fat and connective tissue, so it really works well with a slow and low cook. A good-sized lamb shoulder can take anywhere from 3½ to 6 hours depending on the size, how the animal was raised, the fat content, and other factors. It loves a good basting: this helps keep the joint nice and moist and adds layers of flavour. Let's get to it.

✎ SERVES 8-12

🍖 BBQ SET-UP

Offset firebox or proper smoker (or lonely island technique). Seasoned wood chunks

2–3kg (4lb 4oz–6lb 10oz) lamb shoulder joint, at room temperature

2 tbsp olive oil

2 large dirty onions (see p134)

8–12 large flour tortilla wraps

For the rub

1 tbsp salt

1 tbsp pepper

1 tbsp garlic granules

1 tbsp onion granules

1 tbsp dried oregano

1 tbsp dried thyme

1 tbsp chilli flakes

You need to get your cooker to 120–130°C (250–265°F). For more help on this, see Controlling the Heat on page 12.

Take the lamb shoulder out of the fridge at least an hour before the cook – it's got to be at room temperature when you put it on the grill. Take a sharp knife and lightly score the fat. You are creating more surface area for the rub and basting sauce. Plus, you are giving the fat a bit of a head-start as it slow-cooks and renders down, flavouring the meat.

Put all the rub ingredients into a bowl and mix well. Massage the olive oil all over the scored lamb shoulder, then rub your meat liberally with the seasonings.

Place the joint into the cooker/firebox, or as far away from the heat source as possible if you are using the lonely island technique. Add seasoned wood chunks to your fuel, put the lid on, and slow-cook that baby!

Make the baste by combining the water, vinegar and apple juice. Do not touch the lamb for the first hour; this will help create a tangy crust and keep the moisture in. After the first hour, baste the lamb, then baste again every 45 minutes or so. Cook your dirty onions (see p134) while the lamb is doing its thang. Don't forget to keep your fuel topped up. Go to page 16 for advice on adding fuel.

The lamb is done when it's done. There is no exact timing. You'll need to keep an eye on the joint and do some prodding.

Recipe continues...

For the basting sauce

200ml (7fl oz/generous ¾ cup) water

100ml (3½fl oz/scant ½ cup) red wine vinegar

100ml (3½fl oz/scant ½ cup) apple juice

For the wrap sauce

4 chillies

200ml (7fl oz/generous ¾ cup) plain yogurt

2 tbsp honey

Juice of 1 lemon

1 tbsp tahini

2 tbsp chopped mint leaves, plus 1 tbsp to garnish

1 chilli, to garnish

Recipe continued from p54

There should be a bit of give when you touch the meat and you want to see the meat pulling away from the bone.

When the meat starts to fall off the bone, then you have a major success story. Phone the neighbours, call the kids, wake up your grandma – it's time to celebrate.

Rest the lamb under loose foil for 30 minutes.

While the lamb is resting, make your wrap sauce.

Dirty-cook the chillies by placing them on the used coals. Keep turning until charred. Remove and let them cool.

Chop two of the chillies for the sauce and save two for serving. Add the chopped chillies to the yogurt, along with the honey, lemon juice, tahini and mint leaves.

Peel the cooled dirty onions and roughly chop. Add them to the wrap sauce. Have a taste. Pretty ding dong dang tasty, right?

Pull your meat! Tongs and a fork work well here. You're looking for nice chunks of tender meat with a crispy smoky outside crust.

Quickly toast the tortilla wraps. Layer the meat inside, spoon on the wrap sauce and garnish with a few mint leaves. Add the remaining chillies for extra heat. And get some aioli (see p70) on there too, if you like. Enjoy!

BABY BACK RIBS WITH SZECHUAN MOPPING SAUCE

Get in my belly! Who doesn't love baby back ribs? Ok, so there's a good portion of the planet that doesn't eat meat or pork. More for us! I love digging into a rack of baby backs. Sweet, succulent, juicy meat. The rib muscles near the baby back don't do much work so are super tender. But, because they are smaller, they can dry out if you aren't careful. The key is slow and low love and slatherings of the mopping sauce. If you've been exposed to the Szechuan pepper before, then you are familiar with the numbing feeling. It's almost got a super peppery novocaine vibe to it. The best place to find these little gems is online or in a supermarket with a good world food section.

🍴 SERVES 4

🍖 BBQ SET-UP

Offset firebox or proper smoker (or lonely island technique). Seasoned fruit wood chunks

2 racks of baby back ribs

For the rub

2 tbsp smoked paprika

1 tsp ground allspice

1 tbsp garlic granules

1 tbsp sea salt

1 tsp crushed Szechuan peppercorns

1 tsp mild chilli powder

1 tsp dried oregano

Get your ribs out the fridge an hour before the cook so that they reach room temperature. Putting cold ribs into a smoker only brings the cooker's temperature down and you battle to bring it back up.

Get your smoker to 110°C (230°F) and put some lovely seasoned sweet wood on the coals. For more help on this, see Controlling the Heat on page 12.

The membrane! There are a couple of schools of thought on the membrane. I always used to remove it, as I wanted to penetrate the meat with as much flavour as possible from the rub and mopping sauce. But over the last couple of years, I've been leaving the membrane on as it can help to keep the meat moist and juicy, and also goof-proof your cooking. The last thing you want is a dry rib. The membrane usually flakes off near the end of the cook anyway. It's really your call. You can deal with it before the cook or before you eat.

Put the rub ingredients in a bowl. Mix well. Reserve a couple of tablespoonfuls for the mopping sauce and the garnish, then sprinkle and rub the tasty concoction all over your baby backs.

Recipe continues...

1 tsp dried thyme

1 tsp English mustard
  powder

For the mopping sauce

250ml (9fl oz/generous
  1 cup) cider vinegar

250ml (9fl oz/generous
  1 cup) water

100ml (3½fl oz/scant
  ½ cup) apple juice

1 tbsp Szechuan
  peppercorns

1 tbsp of the rub

Recipe continued from p58

Get your baby backs into the cooker, rib side down on the indirect heat, and slow-cook for at least an hour. You want the wood smoke to oxidize with the rub and meat to start creating a bark. After about 1–1½ hours, you'll see that the fat and connective tissue will start to break down. Your ribs should go from looking dry to a bit oily as the fats start to render. If your ribs haven't hit that sweet spot after 1½ hours, increase the temperature by about 8–10°C (15–20°F) until you get there. For more help on this, see Controlling the Heat on page 12. And head to page 16 for advice on adding fuel.

After the fat has rendered, you need to mop. Get that mopping sauce made. Mix the vinegar, water, apple juice, Szechuan peppercorns (whole) and reserved tablespoon of rub, and mix together in a metal bowl. I like to place the bowl inside the smoker so it heats up and all the flavours fuse together. Plus, it adds moisture to the cook.

Don't baste until the fat has rendered, but once it has, baste those ribs every 30 minutes, but make sure you don't let the hot air out any more than you have to. You need that chemical reaction to happen where the fat and connective tissues break down. If you are looking, it ain't cooking.

When the ribs are ready, you want to see a mahogany colour from the oxidation of the meat and – the most important thing – the meat dance. Basically, a wobble or bend in the ribs. When the ribs are raw, they will be very loose and bendy, then, as you cook them, the ribs will stiffen up. After a couple of hours, the connective tissues and fats break down and the ribs loosen up again to give you the bend. Use your tongs to bend the ribs and check on how forgiving they are. You can also push your finger in between the rib bones to see how tender the meat is. They are done when the meat gives a little. The thing with slow and low cooking is that there's no precise time on when your food is ready to eat. BBQ is done when it's done. These ribs usually take around 3–4 hours.

Slice the ribs and serve. They will be incredible the way they are. Pure! Or, you can sprinkle a bit of the dry rub onto the ribs for that Memphis dry rub taste sensation. And if you need a sauce, these work with the Alabama White Sauce (see p83) or T-Bone's BBQ Sauce (see p175).

SMOKED TURKEY WINGS

Everyone likes a chicken wing. So, how about super-sizing that baby by smoking a turkey wing? Christmas came early and it had wings! This recipe will take a few days to ace, so make sure you plan ahead and get enough beer and bourbon in. There is actually bourbon in the brine but you don't need to add it if you don't want to – you're the boss of your destiny!

SERVES 4

BBQ SET-UP

Offset firebox or proper smoker (or lonely island technique). Seasoned wood chunks

8 turkey wings, split into drumsticks and winglets

For the bourbon brine

1 litre (35fl oz/4¼ cups) water

150g (5½oz/⅔ cup) fine salt

110g (3¾oz/½ cup) brown sugar

200ml (7fl oz/generous ¾ cup) bourbon (optional)

10 garlic cloves, crushed

Zest and juice of 2 lemons

2 tbsp peppercorns

2 tbsp coriander seeds

4 star anise

15 whole cloves

3 red chillies, halved

Large bunch of thyme, rosemary, sage and parsley stems

1kg (2lb 4oz) ice

You will need a large lidded container that can hold all the wings and also fit into your fridge.

First make the brine. Place all the ingredients except the ice into a large saucepan and bring to the boil. Simmer and stir for a couple of minutes until the sugar and salt dissolve. Pull the pan off the cooker and add the ice. Stir and leave to cool.

When the brine is cool, put the turkey wings into the container, pour on the brine, cover with a lid and place in the fridge. Brining the wings is best done overnight, but you can do it first thing in the morning – just make sure you brine them for at least 4–5 hours.

Get your smoker rocking to 125°C (260°F) and put a small tray of water near the firebox end. If you're using a kettle-style cooker, add the tray on the grill near the coals.

Remove your wings from the brine and dry out on some kitchen (paper) towel.

Make your rub. Throw all the ingredients into a mixing bowl and create a mosh pit of flavour! Sprinkle over the dried wings and give them a good rub.

Get the wings straight into the smoker and go slow and low for 3–5 hours. Go to page 16 for advice on adding fuel.

Whisk together the baste ingredients in a bowl. About 1–2 hours into the cook, use a silicon brush to baste the legs every hour, turning them each time you baste. This will help them to develop a really tangy crust.

Recipe continues...

For the rub

1 tbsp sea salt

2 tsp black pepper

2 tsp garlic granules

2 tsp onion granules

2 tsp paprika

2 tsp chilli flakes

2 tsp brown sugar

For the baste

2 tbsp chilli flakes

200ml (7fl oz/generous ¾ cup) cider vinegar

200ml (7fl oz/generous ¾ cup) water

1 tbsp brown sugar

Recipe continued from p65

After the wings are cooked through, tender and beautiful, remove from the smoker and rest on a tray. If you're using a temperature probe, you're looking for 72°C (162°F).

Once cooked, you can glaze them on a hot grill with some T-Bone's BBQ Sauce (see p175) or even Alabama White Sauce (see p83). Don't tell anyone but you could even deep-fry them back in your kitchen in a deep-fat fryer to get that beautiful crispy skin... I told you not to tell anyone!

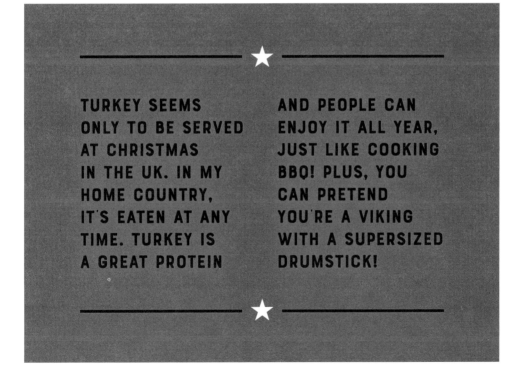

TURKEY SEEMS ONLY TO BE SERVED AT CHRISTMAS IN THE UK. IN MY HOME COUNTRY, IT'S EATEN AT ANY TIME. TURKEY IS A GREAT PROTEIN AND PEOPLE CAN ENJOY IT ALL YEAR, JUST LIKE COOKING BBQ! PLUS, YOU CAN PRETEND YOU'RE A VIKING WITH A SUPERSIZED DRUMSTICK!

ORANGE-SMOKED TROUT

We've used many woods in our smokers on the festival circuit. One of our favourites is the seasoned orange tree wood from Seville, Spain. Our charcoal maker and firebox manager, Matt Williams, turned up with a pallet of the stuff for our biggest festival of the summer, The Big Feastival. It went brilliantly with pork and chicken and it goes splendidly with fish. Orange-smoked fish is incredible – I find that there's a bitter sweetness reminiscent of marmalade. This is ideal served in a salad.

🔪 **SERVES 3-4**

🍖 **BBQ SET-UP**
Offset firebox or proper smoker (or lonely island technique). Seasoned fruit wood chunks, ideally orange

1 whole trout (about 800g–1kg/1lb 12oz–2lb 4oz), gutted, scaled and cleaned, skin on

For the smoking mix

100g (3½oz/½ cup) dark brown sugar

100g (3½oz/scant ½ cup) rice

Zest of 1 orange (if you can't get orange wood), peeled or grated

For the salad

2 broccoli stems, sliced

1 fennel bulb, thinly sliced

1 tsp vegetable oil

200g (7oz) watercress or lamb's lettuce.

1 orange, peeled and segmented

For the mustard dressing

2 tbsp wholegrain mustard

5 tbsp rapeseed oil

1 tbsp honey

2 tbsp balsamic vinegar

Sea salt and black pepper

Get your cooker fired up to 125ºC (260ºF) and dry off your trout with kitchen (paper) towel.

Using a few sheets of foil, make a rough tray with sides. Combine the smoking mix in a bowl and pour into the foil tray.

Place the foil tray on the direct heat, get your trout in the tray, then put the cooker lid on. Leave to smoke for 15–20 minutes until just cooked through. When it is cooked, use a spatula/ fish slice to slide it off the foil tray and onto a board. Leave to rest for 10 minutes under some foil.

While the trout is resting, you can make a salad to go with the fish. Remove the foil tray from the smoker with a pair of tongs. Rub the broccoli and fennel slices with the vegetable oil and char on the grill. Then remove and set aside.

Make up a salad with the watercress leaves, orange segments, broccoli and fennel.

Shake the mustard dressing ingredients in a jar until mixed.

When the trout is rested, carefully peel off the skin with the back of a knife, revealing the flesh. Using two forks, remove the cooked flesh in nice chunks and serve on top of the salad. Drizzle the dressing over the top.

SMOKED GARLIC (FOR AIOLI & BUTTER)

★ ★

Smoked garlic makes an awesome foundation for building a recipe and adding undiscovered depths of flavour – smoke a batch and keep them for the recipes in the book, they keep for 1–2 months. I normally smoke garlic at the end of a cookout, as there's usually some leftover coals still burning in the cooker. I like to throw a log of seasoned smoking wood or a couple of chunks straight onto the coals and leave the garlic overnight. Cooking while sleeping – that is what I'm all about. Or you can get a small bed of coals going in the morning.

🏮 BBQ SET-UP

Offset firebox or proper smoker (or lonely island technique). Seasoned wood chunks

As much large-clove garlic as you'd like to smoke (ideally new season/wet garlic)

For the aioli

4 bulbs of smoked large-clove garlic

Juice of 1 lemon

2 tsp salt

300ml (10½fl oz/1¼ cups) vegetable oil

Water, to loosen

Place your garlic bulbs into your cooker as far away from the coals as possible. You don't want much heat here, just a warm blanket of sleepy smoke, so add a couple of seasoned smoking wood chunks onto the coals and get your smoke rocking. Cover or close the lid and have a last beer before bed. In the morning, make a strong cup of coffee and open up your smoker. Inside you will find chestnut coloured bulbs of smoked garlic. Remove and store these little pillows of smokiness in the fridge for later or even a couple of weeks away.

You can use these babies in many recipes but these two are a couple of great little ideas for using this amazing smoked garlic flavour.

To make the aioli... Peel the smoked garlic and put the cloves into a bowl or pestle and mortar. Add in the lemon juice and salt, and crush until you have a smooth paste.

Gradually pour in the oil, mixing each time until smooth and gooey – it should be almost like mayonnaise. If it is really thick, mix in a little water to loosen. This is one punchy mother$%£$@r and a superb condiment for a burger.

Recipe continues...

For the butter

2 bulbs of smoked large-clove garlic

250g (9oz) butter, softened

2 tbsp your favourite herb(s), such as rosemary and thyme, finely chopped (optional)

Pinch of salt (if using unsalted butter)

Zest of ½ lemon

Recipe continued from p70

And now for the butter. Peel the smoked garlic and crush the cloves a bowl or pestle and mortar. Mix the garlic into the softened butter, along with your favourite herb(s), the lemon zest and salt (if using), and whip well. Get all those ingredients evenly spread throughout the butter.

Now, lay out a sheet of cling film (plastic wrap) on a work surface. Spoon the butter out into a long sausage. Roll the cling wrap into a super-tight butter roll, twist the ends closed and chill in the fridge. The butter will be good for a couple of weeks or you can freeze to make it last longer. Cut off a disc when you need it. Every steak in the world loves this butter.

Go Team Awesome!

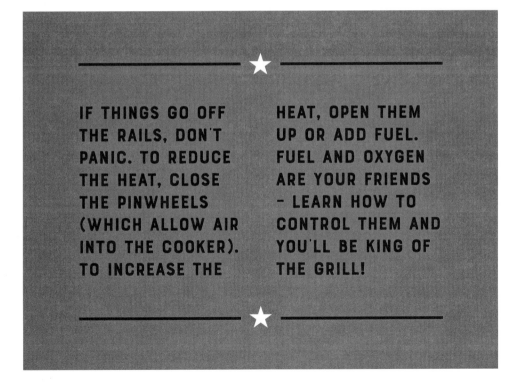

IF THINGS GO OFF THE RAILS, DON'T PANIC. TO REDUCE THE HEAT, CLOSE THE PINWHEELS (WHICH ALLOW AIR INTO THE COOKER). TO INCREASE THE HEAT, OPEN THEM UP OR ADD FUEL. FUEL AND OXYGEN ARE YOUR FRIENDS - LEARN HOW TO CONTROL THEM AND YOU'LL BE KING OF THE GRILL!

KEEP ON GRILLIN' IN THE FREE WORLD

IF YOU'RE AFTER SIMPLE AND SATISFYING BURGERS, WINGS, SEAFOOD AND MORE, THEN THIS IS THE CHAPTER FOR YOU!

THE ULTIMATE CHEESEBURGER

★ ★

The DJ BBQ crew cook a lot of burgers. I reckon each summer we grill around 8,000 burgers over live fire. I've hosted many burger competitions and food festivals and seen many different techniques, ranging from classic to downright weird. I've spent the last 40 years perfecting this burger. I hope you are ready to achieve awesomeness because you are about to invite a wonderful cheeseburger to that party in your mouth. This is the blend that we believe is perfect. Many people won't have access to a butcher or these cuts of meat, so just go for a decent fatty beef mince (ground beef). The more fat, the better. Minimum 20% fat.

✎ SERVES 4

♜ BBQ SET-UP
Half and half technique. You will need a metal cloche

For the beef mince (ground beef)

You can ask your butcher to prepare this mix of cuts but if you want to do it yourself, here are the weights as well as the percentages to make 1kg (2lb 4oz) beef mince (ground beef). Simply put all the meat through a coarse grain mincer (meat grinder.

450g (1lb) chuck (45%)

150g (5½oz) Flank (15%)

150g (5½oz) Brisket (15%)

100g (3½oz) short rib (10%)

100g (3½oz) aged beef fat (10%)

50g (1¾oz) bone marrow (5%)

First, get all of your toppings ready. Start by making the smoked garlic mayo by mixing the grated horseradish, smoked garlic, lemon juice and mayonnaise in a bowl. Set aside.

Mix the chopped dirty onion with the cider vinegar, then season with a pinch of sea salt and set aside.

For the seasoning salt, mix all the dried ingredients together in a bowl. Get all your veg prepped and have your cheese ready. Finally, get your grill going with a medium hot heat.

Now, it's patty time. You don't want a super-dense patty. A coarse grain on the mince means the fats can render down and flavour the beef patty. Divide the mince into four equal piles. Carefully sculpt each pile into a patty. I like my patty to be about 2.5cm (1 inch) thick. Make sure it is even all round, so there aren't any bits that are fatter than the rest. When creating the patty, I like to see cracks around the edge of the burger – I call these 'fjords of flavour'. As the fats render down, they will cascade down these fjords and flavour the patty.

Recipe continues...

For the smoked garlic mayo

2.5cm (1 inch) fresh horseradish root, grated (shredded)

4 smoked garlic cloves, peeled and crushed (see p70)

Juice of ½ lemon

100ml (3½fl oz/½ cup) mayonnaise

For the dirty onions

1 big dirty onion (see p134), chopped

2 tbsp cider vinegar

Pinch of sea salt

For the seasoning salt

1 tbsp sea salt

1 tsp black pepper

½ tsp onion granules

½ tsp garlic granules

To serve

4 slices of Monterey Jack cheese

4 slices of burger cheese (the orange stuff)

8 slices of smoked dry cured streaky bacon

4 brioche-style burger bun, halved

1 Romaine lettuce, separated into leaves

1 ripe tomato (preferably beef), sliced

Recipe continued from p77

Sprinkle the seasoning salt onto both sides of the patties and place them over direct heat. When the patties come away from the grill easily, then it's time to flip. Flip again when the grill releases your patties on the other side, and keep flipping every 1–2 minutes until the burgers are cooked through.

If you get flare-ups and it's getting out of hand, move the patties to the indirect side, so you can calm things down. Plus, this gives the burger a chance to do some more cooking on the inside.

Once the burgers are about three-quarters done (about 50°C/122°F), lay a slice of both types of cheese in a cross on each patty and place the cloche over the burgers to melt the cheese quickly.

Move the burger to the indirect side just before it's hit the internal temperature you are after. I like my burger to be cooked medium-rare (55°C/131°F).

As soon as you move the burgers over, get the bacon on the direct heat along with the bun halves, cut side down. When the bacon and the buns have a nice crispy char, remove everything onto a board ready to assemble.

To assemble, lay out the bottom half of the bun, spread a dollop of the smoked garlic mayo on it, followed by a piece of lettuce. Now it's time for the main event! Cast that grilled, cheesy, slab of meaty beef ass down on top of the lettuce, like Thor casting thunderbolts into Hades. Finish off with the bacon, tomato and dirty onions. All you need to do now is pop that toasted bun on top to seal the deal. Then, suddenly, bam! You have made the ultimate cheeseburger!

WHOLE GRILLED SEA BASS

I spend a lot of time with my three sons down in the Algarve, Portugal. I truly believe that the Portuguese are some of the best fish grillers in the world. A couple of my favourite fish joints are in Lagos and Burgau. If you ever find yourself in Lagos, try finding Escondidinho ('The Hidden Place'). Its mixed fish grill is a must for any fan of seafood. I learned a great technique from their pitmaster, Phil the Pirate: he keeps a bucket of charcoal ash near the grill so he can suffocate his fuel if it gets out of hand. Grilling fish is an art. It's very easy for the fish to stick to the grill. It's really easy to burn the fish on the outside while the inside is still raw. You need a medium heat so the fish cooks perfectly throughout. Grilled sea bass, or robalo grelhado, is one of the most popular dishes in Portugal. Here's my take on this classic.

SERVES 4

BBQ SET-UP
Heat canyon or half and half technique

1 whole sea bass (about 1.5kg/3lb 5oz), gutted, scaled and cleaned

3 garlic cloves, crushed or chopped

Handful of parsley leaves, chopped

½ lemon, cut into thin wedges

Sea salt

For the sauce
50g (1¾oz) butter

Juice of 1 lemon

1 tbsp capers

First, get that grill spotless and seasoned with vegetable oil (see p11). This will help stop the fish from sticking.

Next, thoroughly dry the fish with kitchen (paper) towel. This also helps prevent the fish from sticking. Using a sharp knife, lightly score the skin every 2.5cm (1 inch).

Stuff the cavity with the garlic, parsley and lemon wedges, and season the stuffing with salt. Give the fish another dry with some kitchen towel, and place on the grill in between the two coal beds on the indirect heat.

Grill the fish for at least 5–7 minutes until the skin starts to crisp up and releases from the grill. You need either a really wide metal fish slice or two normal spatulas to do the flip. Gently tease the skin off the grill and turn the fish onto the other side. Season with salt and keep on cooking. Once the skin releases, turn the fish again and season. You are looking for a slightly crispy skin and for the flesh to be cooked all the way to the bone. The last thing you want is that mucousy stuff around the bone. Stick a thermometer into the fattest part of the fish and, as soon as it hits 58°C (136°F), pull it off to rest for 5 minutes.

While the fish is resting, put a small frying pan (skillet) over the direct heat and add the butter, lemon juice and capers for your sauce. When it is all sizzling, spoon it over the rested fish and serve up on a pro Geoff Rowley skateboard deck.

ALABAMA WHITE SAUCE CHICKEN

★ ★

Every town, county and state in the United States has their preferred BBQ sauce. Some are tomato- or mustard-based, some are sweet and others are tangy. And some – like Alabama's famous white sauce – are creamy *and* tangy. Big Bob Gibson put the sauce on the map in the early part of the 20th century and now it can be found in numerous BBQ joints across America. I love tangy, and this definitely has some tang! It's been my most popular dish at cookouts – tried and tested deliciousness.

✎ **SERVES 4**

🍖 **BBQ SET-UP**
   Half and half technique

1 chicken, about 1.5kg
   (3lb 5oz), jointed into
   8 pieces (thighs,
   drumsticks, wings
   and breasts)

**For the Alabama white
   sauce**
250g (9oz/generous
   1 cup) mayonnaise
175ml (6fl oz/¾ cup) cider
   vinegar
Juice of ½ lemon
1cm (½ inch) fresh
   horseradish root,
   grated (shredded)
1 tsp paprika or chilli flakes
   (if you want to spice it up)
1 tbsp Worcestershire sauce
2 tbsp black pepper
   (or more – this recipe
   loves pepper)
1 tbsp sea salt

For the sauce, combine all the ingredients in a large bowl and whisk till smooth. Some people like to make a thick version of this sauce to serve with the cooked chicken as a dip, and others just use it as a thin basting sauce. I do both! So, put a couple of tablespoons of the sauce aside, add more mayo to thicken, and serve in a small bowl.

Now you need to get your chicken cooking. Once your coals are ready, lay the chicken skin-side down over the direct heat and get some colour rocking on it. Cook for about 15 minutes until it is slightly golden in colour on the outside. You'll need to turn it a couple of times during that 15 mintutes.

Keep an eye on the chicken because when the fat breaks down and starts to drip on the coals, there will be lots of flare-ups and it can burn. If it gets out of hand, move the chicken to the indirect side of the grill to mellow out for a bit. Once you have a slight golden colour all over the chicken, move the pieces to the indirect side and put the lid on to retain the heat and keep the chicken cooking.

Now the beauty of this white sauce is that there's no sugar, which means you can baste your meat much earlier in the cook – start basting about halfway or two-thirds into your cook. Your standard tomato/vinegar/sugar-based BBQ sauces should be added near the end of the cook, so the sugar doesn't burn. (Having said that, if you've made your own mayo, it's best to use the sauce near the end too, as it won't like the heat and will split.)

Recipe continues...

Recipe continued from p83

One by one, remove each piece of chicken from the grill, dip it into the tasty white sauce, and place back onto the indirect side of the grill. Place the lid back onto the cooker and cook for a couple more minutes to cook the glaze.

As you approach the end of your cook, give the chicken another dip and repeat the process (dip, put it back on the indirect side, cook for a couple of minutes). Heck, you can even go for a triple dip, cooking the glaze each time. It's your cookout – get crazy!

As soon as the internal temperature of the chicken is 72°C (162°F), then you can remove it from the heat. Rest uncovered for 10 minutes, before serving with the thickened white sauce for dipping.

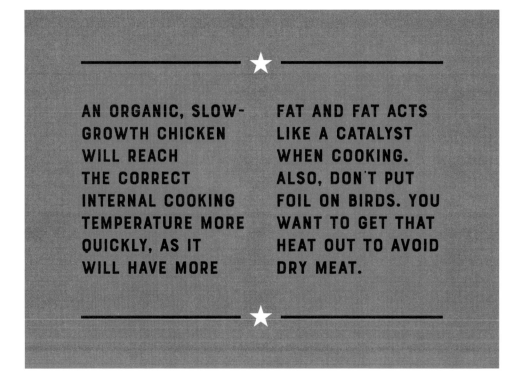

AN ORGANIC, SLOW-GROWTH CHICKEN WILL REACH THE CORRECT INTERNAL COOKING TEMPERATURE MORE QUICKLY, AS IT WILL HAVE MORE FAT AND FAT ACTS LIKE A CATALYST WHEN COOKING. ALSO, DON'T PUT FOIL ON BIRDS. YOU WANT TO GET THAT HEAT OUT TO AVOID DRY MEAT.

GRILLED CHICKEN HEART ATTACKS

Considering that 'chicken' is the most Googled food in the world, chicken hearts are one of the most under-used pieces of meat. These chicken hearts are incredible straight on the grill, finished with T-Bone's sauce (see p175). They are so moreish I sometimes end up smashing half of the tangy hearts before I even leave the grill.

✎ SERVES 4

♨ BBQ SET-UP
Half and half technique. You will also need 4 metal skewers

20 chicken hearts

1 tsp vegetable oil

4 tbsp T-Bone's BBQ sauce (see p175)

For the rub
1 tbsp smoked paprika

1 tsp dried oregano

1 tsp sumac

1 tsp flaked salt

Dry the chicken hearts with kitchen (paper) towel and place in a mixing bowl. Add the oil and lightly coat the hearts.

Mix the ingredients for the rub together in a small bowl and pour over the hearts. Rub the mix into the hearts, then thread them onto the skewers.

Get the skewers straight over the direct heat and get them grilling. Once you have a golden colour, turn the skewers and keep going. You will need to grill these for about 5 minutes until cooked though and you have a nice crust all round.

Once they're cooked, use a silicon brush to glaze the hearts with the sauce and grill for another couple of minutes, turning all the time.

The sauce will caramelize really quickly. As soon as you have a light char, remove the skewers and serve the hearts straightaway.

BUTTERFLIED WILD VENISON HAUNCH IN OYSTER SAUCE

★ ★

The UK has been making sauces with oysters since the early 19th century... possibly longer. The oyster flavour really complements the gamey red meat of venison and beef. I got the idea for this recipe about 10 years ago and for some reason I haven't unleashed it until now! We've been hosting a live fire course with our friends at Hunter Gather Cook. We teach the good people of Europe how to make fire, handle fire, maintain fire and cook with fire, all with a medley of wild ingredients. And luckily for me, I once walked away with a gorgeous wild fallow venison haunch. We butterflied that beautiful hunk of meat, marinated it overnight, and grilled it. I can honestly say that it was one of the best things I've tasted in the last decade. I'm giving this recipe a Chinese twist as Chinese oyster sauce is readily available and gives that amazing oyster flavour along with a rich sweetness that goes brilliantly with game.

✎ **SERVES 8-10**

🍖 **BBQ SET-UP**
Half and half technique

Haunch of wild venison, butterflied and scored, with most of the fatty sinew removed (ask your butcher to do this for you)

Sesame seeds, to garnish

For the marinade

150ml (5fl oz/scant ⅔ cup) oyster sauce

8 garlic cloves, chopped

5cm (2 inches) ginger, peeled and chopped

50ml (1¾fl oz/scant ¼ cup) soy sauce

50ml (1¾fl oz/scant ¼ cup) rice vinegar

2 tbsp sesame oil

Make up the marinade by mixing all the ingredients together in a bowl.

Place the venison haunch in a roasting tin (pan), big enough so that it fits comfortably. Rub the meat with the marinade, making sure you get it into all the nooks and crannies. Cover with cling film (plastic wrap) and leave to take on the intense flavour overnight. You know this is gonna be badass, because that flavour will hit your nostrils as soon as it's spread on your meat!

When you're about half an hour from eating, slap your marinated haunch on the direct heat and get the rich caramelization going. Once you have that dark caramelization all over the slab, move the venison to the indirect side, you want it to cook through. So put the grill lid on and suffocate the fuel by closing the pinwheels (air vents).

Leave it to roast very slowly until it's blushing medium−rare, about 55°C (131°F). Rest on a board for about 10 minutes and slice to enjoy.

This is a great main event dish. The meat and marinade does the talking. If you have any leftovers, slice them thin with chopped spring onions (scallions), mayo and throw them in a wrap.

GRILLED HALLOUMI BURGER WITH SMASHED AVOCADO

Every good pitmaster needs a solid veggie burger in their arsenal. But this recipe is also a favourite with my meat-eating brethren – it is super-simple, quick to make and packed with flavour.

🍴 **SERVES 4**

🍖 **BBQ SET-UP**
   Target technique

For the seasoning

1 tsp sumac

Pinch of cayenne pepper

1 tsp paprika

For the smashed avocado

2 super-ripe avocados

Juice of 1 lime

For the burgers

4 x halloumi cheese slices, 2cm (¾ inch) thick

Olive oil, for drizzling

4 burger buns (I like using brioche or demi-brioche)

Handful of mint leaves, chopped

Pomegranate molasses, to drizzle

2 ripe tomatoes (preferably beef), sliced

Bunch of rocket (arugula)

Put all the seasoning spices in a bowl and mix well.

Halve the avocados, remove the pits and, using a large spoon, pull the ripe flesh away from the skin and empty into a bowl. Using the back of a large spoon, smash the avocado to a chunky paste. Pour in the lime juice, give it a light mix and set aside.

Lay the halloumi slabs on a plate and drizzle olive oil on both sides. Lightly sprinkle the seasoning mix all over the cheese.

Once seasoned, place the slabs over direct heat and grill for a couple minutes on one side until you have some lovely golden grill marks. Flip and repeat. Everything happens pretty quickly, so this is a good time to toast your burger buns on the grill.

Assembly time! Spoon the avocado onto the four bun bases. Sprinkle the chopped mint onto the avocado, then place the halloumi steaks on top. Next, drizzle the pomegranate molasses onto the halloumi. Top that with the tomato slices and rocket.

Serve and watch your friends' eyes widen with excitement.

AIN'T NOTHIN BUT A CHICKEN WING

★ ★

This recipe is all about the tastiest part of the chicken – the almighty wing! (Though we can all agree, the thigh runs a close second in flavour.) The chicken needs marinating overnight for extra delicious flavour, but a quick rub with the marinade works well if you're short on time.

🍴 SERVES 4

🍖 BBQ SET-UP
Half and half technique. Seasoned wood chunks, preferably a fruit wood

1kg (2lb 4oz) chicken wings

2 tbsp vegetable oil

For the rub

1 tbsp sea salt

2 tsp black pepper

2 tsp garlic granules

2 tsp onion granules

2 tsp paprika

2 tsp dried thyme

First, prepare the chicken wings. Start by removing the tips with a sharp knife. Then, make a slit on the underneath of the wing, cutting the flap of skin in half to allow the two halves to spread out easily.

Prepare the rub by mixing all the ingredients together in a small bowl.

Rub the chicken wings evenly all over with the oil and lay out on a large tray. Dust the rub over the wings on both sides, creating a nice even coating of wingtacular brilliance. Leave to marinate overnight.

Add the wood chunks right up to the edge of the coals and place the wings on the indirect side of the grill above the wood. Place a lid on and smoke the wings at around 120°C (250°F) for 1½ hours until cooked through and nice and smoky. If you're using a temperature probe, you're looking for 72°C (162°F).

These are excellent to eat as they are. But you can take them to the next level by crisping them up over the direct heat. You can also glaze them (after crisping up) with the Alabama White Sauce (see p83) or T-Bone's BBQ Sauce (see p175).

ZA'ATAR AND HONEY GLAZED SPATCHCOCK CHICKEN

This is one of my new favourites. Za'atar originated in the Middle East and is normally used on pittas and flatbreads with olive oil. It's also sprinkled onto hummus. I love to use it as a spice rub when grilling chicken. It's got a lovely earthy and citrusy taste. Deep, rich and delicious. The first time I experienced za'atar was when I went snowboarding in Lebanon in 2000. I was blown away by the landscape, the mountains and, of course, the food.

✎ SERVES 2-4

🔥 BBQ SET-UP
Half and half technique

1 chicken, about 1.5kg (3lb 5oz)

Olive oil

Honey, to glaze

For the za'atar rub

1 tbsp sesame seeds, toasted

1 tbsp dried thyme

1 tbsp sumac

1 tbsp sea salt

You can spatchcock the chicken yourself but, if you don't want to, your butcher can always do it for you.

Place your chicken on a chopping board breast side down, legs facing you. Using meat scissors (shears), open the chicken up by cutting on one side of the parson's nose (tail) and all along the spine to the neck end. Then, cut all the way along the spine on the other side of the parson's nose to detach the spine completely. Turn the chicken over and flatten it with the palm of your hand. It is now ready to be rubbed with flavour.

Mix all the rub ingredients in a bowl.

We are using a thin film of olive oil as the glue for the rub, but you want to use a very small amount. The best way to nail this recipe is to rub olive oil into your hands, then rub your hands over the chicken until it's very slightly oily.

Then, sprinkle the za'atar rub all over the chicken.

Place the chicken skin side down over a direct heat. Once the chicken has a light char, carefully turn the bird bone side down. If the skin sticks, then use a spatula to gently prise the chicken off without tearing.

Recipe continues...

Recipe continued from p94

Now you've got some babysitting – or chicken-sitting – to do. You'll need to keep the chicken over the direct heat for around 10 minutes. The fats will render down and you'll get occasional flare-ups. If they get too intense, move the chicken to the indirect side. Once you have a nice brown crust on the chicken, place it on the indirect side and put the lid on the cooker.

Cook for 35 minutes–1 hour. Stick a temperature probe into the thickest part of the thigh and once it hits 67–70ºC (153–158ºF), you can drizzle some honey onto the skin for a sweet and savoury taste sensation. Once the chicken hits 72ºC (162ºF), remove it from the heat and let it rest on a board for 10–15 minutes before serving. Serve with Babaganoush (see p140) and some toasted sourghdough for an epic feast.

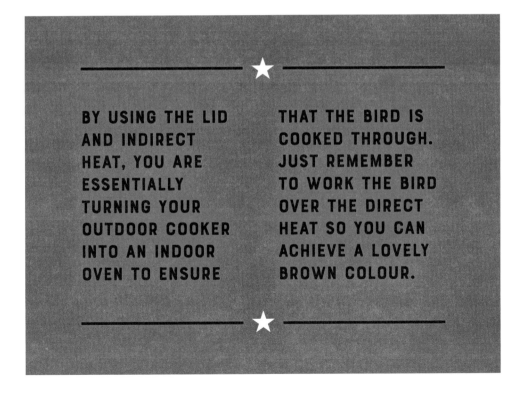

BY USING THE LID AND INDIRECT HEAT, YOU ARE ESSENTIALLY TURNING YOUR OUTDOOR COOKER INTO AN INDOOR OVEN TO ENSURE THAT THE BIRD IS COOKED THROUGH. JUST REMEMBER TO WORK THE BIRD OVER THE DIRECT HEAT SO YOU CAN ACHIEVE A LOVELY BROWN COLOUR.

PRAWN TACOS WITH GRILLED WATERMELON SALSA

Who said you couldn't grill watermelon? Well, pretty much everyone. But I started doing this recipe one summer and it became an instant hit. When I did a guest-chef stint at a friend's taco joint called Bad Sports in London, this was the top selling taco of the night. Don't be afraid if the watermelon gets a dark crust, it will disappear when you chop it up.

✎ **SERVES 4-6**

🍴 **BBQ SET-UP**
Half and half technique

12 extra-large tiger prawns, head on, tail shell removed, deveined

1 green or red jalapeño chilli, sliced open lengthways and deseeded

Soft tortilla wraps

Sea salt

For the salsa

2 medium-sized watermelon slices (save the rinds for pickling, see p173)

1 red onion, finely chopped

Handful of coriander (cilantro) leaves, chopped

1 green jalapeño chilli, deseeded and chopped

Juice of 1 lemon

Remove the rind from your watermelon and grill the slices over direct heat until the dark char appears on the red fruit flesh. (You can do this with the rinds on, too, if you prefer.) Once both sides have a good colour, take them off to cool down. Don't worry if bits of the fruit go black. It's all flavour.

Prepare your salsa by mixing the red onion, coriander, chopped chilli and lemon juice in a bowl. When the watermelon has cooled down, give it a chop, add it to the bowl and mix again.

Rub your prawns with the opened chilli and salt, and grill on the direct heat until cooked through, about 5 minutes or the meat is opaque.

When cooked and a little cooled, you can take the heads off the prawns. Then suck the head juice out of the prawn. Yes! You are awesome! Love me some prawn head juice!

Toast the tortilla wraps on the grill. Now it's time to assemble. Fill the wraps with the prawns and top with the salsa. Fold and consume. Then smile, but you don't need to be told that because it will happen involuntarily.

THE PERFECT STEAK
– SMACKED RIBEYE

★ ★

Yup, that's correct. You read it right. The perfect steak. So, what makes steak taste so great? First off it is the cow. A grass-fed cow is going to taste different to one that's been grain-fed. I find there's a sweeter taste to corn- and grain-fed beef, but a much more dynamic flavour to grass-fed beef. I like them both, but prefer grass-fed. I also prefer an animal that has lived a longer life: give me a 10–15-year-old dairy cow and I'm in heaven. Or, in an ideal world, a 4–6-year-old highland from the Isle of Mull off Scotland – that's an animal raised on beautiful hearty foliage like heather and hardened grasses. We can go all super geek on this, so let's get on with the perfect steak. My favourite cut is the ribeye, on the bone or off. The sweetest meat is next to the bone, but you get a more complete caramelization with the bone removed – it's your steak so it's your call!

🔪 SERVES 1-4
(it depends how hungry you are – I can easily share this with 2 or 3 people, but I have friends who can eat this baby all on their own)

🍖 BBQ SET-UP
Half and half technique. If you have a grill with upper levels or one that can be raised up and down, get it set up – you will have greater control

1kg (2lb 4oz) aged ribeye, on or off the bone, at room temperature

Sea salt and black pepper

Get yourself a super-thick cut of ribeye, about 7.5cm (3 inches) thick would be perfect. 'Too thick!' I hear you yell. Well, hold your horses, cowboy, we are getting there. First, make sure it's at room temperature. If you are cooking the ribeye with the bone, skip the next step.

Place the meat on a sturdy surface (I normally place a chopping board on the floor), then, with the back of a good-size frying pan (skillet), smack that thing! Give it a good wallop, then flip it over and do it again. Get that steak to around 4–5cm (1½–2 inches). By doing this, you are creating more surface area. Next, take a sharp knife and lightly cut into the meat, aiming for the fat. If there's a good chunk of fat on the outside, then make a ladder of slices about 1cm (½ inch) apart. Get a pinch of salt and season.

Get a good heat rocking on your BBQ. Place the steak over the direct heat and begin to create that crust. The fats will start to break down and these are going to flavour the meat. I'm not big on grill marks – I just want a perfectly cooked steak – so move that steak around as it cooks. Once it has a good sear on it, flip it over. Again, move it around. Once you have a sear on the flip side, you need to work the perimeter.

Recipe continues...

Recipe continued from p100

If you have a ribeye with a bone, you will need to cook the steak bone side down for a minute or two, depending on the steak, maybe even longer. You'll need to hold it in place with the tongs if it won't stand up on its own. If it does, damn, you got yourself a pretty big steak.

Once you have a good sear all around the edge of the steak, move it away from the intense heat – to the upper grills or the indirect side. That intense heat is there to help you create that crust on the outside. You want to achieve that beautiful Maillard reaction without going too far so it is bitter and burnt. If it looks like it's burning or there are flare-ups, move it away and keep it on the indirect heat. You can always put it back again when the flames have cut back. I keep moving my steak from direct heat to indirect heat until it's perfect. One of the great myths about cooking steak is that you only turn it once.

How do you know when it's perfect? Well, you can use a temperature probe in the thickest part of the steak. I like my ribeye to be medium-rare (50–55°C/122–131°F). That way the fats break down and flavour the meat. You can pull the steak off at 48–49°C (118–120°F) and it will still go up in temperature as it's resting. Or, you can poke the steak. See below!

Once the steak is done, hit it with some freshly cracked pepper and rest on a board. I don't put pepper on at the beginning as it can burn and go acrid. Slice, season with salt, and serve. Congrats! You are awesome! That's what your friends, family and stomach will say.

RARE, MEDIUM OR WELL-DONE?

Here's a great technique for cooking your steak the way you like it. Hold out your hand, palm up, then touch your index finger and thumb together. With the index finger of your other hand, gently poke the fleshy pocket between the bottom of the thumb and your wrist. This is how a rare steak will feel when you prod it.

Touch the thumb and the middle finger together, and press the same spot again and this is how a medium-rare steak will feel.

Touch the thumb and your third finger together, and that fleshy bit under your thumb will feel like a rad steak cooked to medium. Thumb to pinky feels like a well-done steak.

LIVE FIRE FRITTATA

Back in the early 1990s I lived in a ski resort in Vail, Colorado as a snowboard bum. I worked part time at a 24-hour diner called DJ's Diner. We specialized in omelettes, chillies and this dish: 'The Frittata' or fried pasta. It's super-tasty comfort food stuffed full of carbs, veggies and protein – exactly what you need when shredding the rad in the mountains. Make sure you have everything prepped and ready to assemble for the final dish.

✎ SERVES 4

♨ BBQ SET-UP
Half and half technique

2 onions – I like using a red one for sweetness and the classic cooking onion for sharpness, peeled and thickly sliced

1 red, 1 green, 1 yellow (bell) pepper, halved and deseeded

6 smoked bacon rashers (slices)

2 chicken breasts

200g (7oz) spaghetti

3 eggs, beaten within an inch of their life

Vegetable oil, for frying

250g (9oz) Cheddar cheese, grated (shredded)

50g (1¾ oz) Parmesan cheese, grated

Sea salt and black pepper

Get the marinara sauce cooking so it has time to do its flavour-fusing thing. Place a medium saucepan on the grill over the direct heat and pour in the olive oil. Once hot, add the garlic, capers and anchovies. Fry for 2 minutes, then add the tomatoes and oregano. Move to the indirect side and leave to simmer slowly, while you prep your other ingredients. You might want to add a bit of water if the sauce gets too thick.

Meanwhile, stick the onions and peppers on the grill over the direct heat until tender and then set aside. Cook the bacon in the same way until crispy. Rub the chicken breasts with olive oil, season and grill till cooked through (if you're using a temperature probe, you're looking for 72°C/162°F), then leave to cool.

Boil the spaghetti according to the packet instructions (you can do this in the kitchen if it's easier). When the spaghetti is cooked, drain and leave to cool.

Roughly chop the onions and the peppers. Slice and dice the chicken breasts. Roughly chop the crispy bacon.

Place a small frying pan (skillet) with a bit of depth to it on the grill over the direct heat. I like using cast-iron or iron-spun pans as they radiate the best heat for caramelization.

Recipe continues…

For the marinara sauce

4 tbsp olive oil

4 smoked garlic cloves,
peeled and chopped
(see p70)

2 tbsp capers, drained and
roughly chopped

4 canned anchovy fillets,
chopped

2 x 400g (14oz) cans
chopped tomatoes

1 tsp dried oregano

Recipe continued from p104

To make one frittata at a time, take a mixing bowl and throw in about a quarter of cooked spaghetti followed by a quarter of the peppers, onions, chicken and bacon. Add a quarter of the beaten eggs to the bowl and mix.

Drizzle some vegetable oil into the hot pan. Now carefully pour the ingredients from the bowl into the frying pan. Season with salt. Use a spatula to pull the ingredients away from the edge so you create something that looks like a Spanish tortilla. Fry for a couple of minutes until you have a golden-brown crust on the bottom. Use the spatula to check. Once you've got the right colour, carefully flip the frittata over. The egg will start to bind and hold the pasta together. Give the flip side another couple of minutes. Flip one more time, cover with a quarter of the grated Cheddar cheese and set aside to rest while you cook the others.

Once you've cooked all your frittatas, serve with a slathering of marinara sauce and Parmesan. Crack some pepper on top and enjoy your food coma. You can always ski it off.

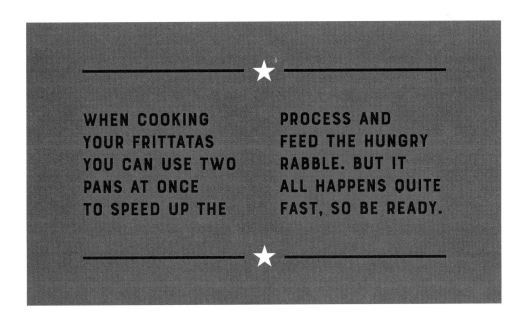

WHEN COOKING YOUR FRITTATAS YOU CAN USE TWO PANS AT ONCE TO SPEED UP THE PROCESS AND FEED THE HUNGRY RABBLE. BUT IT ALL HAPPENS QUITE FAST, SO BE READY.

VEGETARIAN BURGER OF SMOKINESS

★ ★

It can be a challenge to make a tasty veggie burger and there are a lot of recipes that taste like dog's poop. Anyone can cook a decent burger, but the true mark of a good cook is if they can handle veg without the meat crutch. It says a lot about a restaurant if it has a properly tasty veggie burger on its menu, since most of the planet sucks at cooking veggie burgers. That's right, everyone sucked until NOW. I can hear the angels singing and rejoicing as they quaff the ambrosia of awesomeness emanating from this veggie burger. And so it begins... This recipe uses butter beans as a base, which gives a smoother texture than using chickpeas (garbanzo beans) and a really meaty flavour.

🍴 **SERVES 4**

🍖 **BBQ SET-UP**
   Half and half technique

1 dirty onion (see p134)

1 smoked garlic bulb; you'll need 4 cloves (see p70)

2 corn on the cobs in husk (wrap corn in foil if you can't get it in husks)

1 x 400g (14oz) can butter beans, drained and dried out on kitchen (paper) towel

Bunch of oregano, leaves picked and chopped

1 tsp celery salt

1 tsp black pepper

Get your onions cooking in the coals (see Dirty Onions, p134). and your garlic smoked (see Smoked Garlic, p70). After 45 minutes, place the corn on the cobs in the coals and give them 15 minutes, turning regularly. When they are done, take them off and let them cool down in a metal tray.

Once everything is cooked and cooled, slice the sweetcorn kernels off the cobs with a knife. Roughly chop the corn and the dirty onion flesh and four of the smoked garlic cloves (reserve the rest for another recipe).

Crush the beans in a large bowl with a fork until mushy. Then add the corn, garlic and onion, as well as the oregano, celery salt, pepper, 2–3 tablespoons of flour and lemon juice. Bring it all together like a mosh pit. The mix will seem quite wet at this stage.

Put all the flour/spice mix ingredients in a bowl and stir well. Get a frying pan (skillet) nice and hot over direct heat. Liberally dust a board with some of the flour/spice mix.

Recipe continues...

2–3 tbsp plain (all-purpose) flour

Juice of ½ lemon

Vegetable oil, for frying

For the flour/spice mix

50g (1¾ oz) plain (all-purpose) flour

½ tsp paprika

½ tsp cayenne pepper

½ tsp sea salt

½ tsp black pepper

½ tsp garlic granules

½ tsp onion granules

To serve

4 burger buns

Iceberg lettuce, chopped

1 ripe tomato (preferably beef), sliced

Recipe continued from p109

Empty the burger mix onto the floured board and divide into four balls. Using the flour/spice mix to coat. Shape the balls into four patties.

Add vegetable oil to the pan and carefully place each patty into the pan and fry, flipping a couple of times, until you have a nice even golden crust on both sides. This will take some time depending on how hot your pan is – anywhere from 15 to 25 minutes. You are building a tasty crust that will give an awesome crunch with a soft centre. You can always move to the indirect side if the burger needs to cook through.

When the burgers are ready, slice open and toast your buns and serve with lettuce, tomato and your favourite condiment.

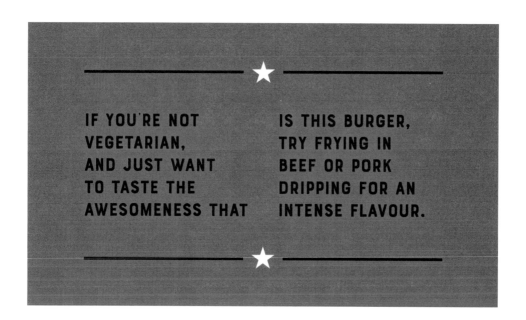

IF YOU'RE NOT VEGETARIAN, AND JUST WANT TO TASTE THE AWESOMENESS THAT IS THIS BURGER, TRY FRYING IN BEEF OR PORK DRIPPING FOR AN INTENSE FLAVOUR.

TOMATO PIE

I spent my summers in Virginia Beach, where me and my grandaddy would fish in the Atlantic Ocean, and me and my grandma would do fish fries and clam bakes. This tomato pie is the perfect side dish for all the above. It also makes a great main event. My vegetarian friends love it when I cook this – it's an all-time favourite.

SERVES 2-4

BBQ SET-UP
Heat canyon technique

Knob of butter

150g (5½oz) mature Cheddar cheese, grated (shredded)

1 onion, grated (shredded)

100g (3½oz/½ cup) mayonnaise

Glug of Worcestershire sauce

1 tsp dried oregano

10 slices of day-old white bread (use a sourdough for next-level deliciousness), crusts removed, cut or ripped into cubes

6–8 ripe tomatoes, ends removed, sliced

1 spring onion (scallion), sliced

1 red chilli, sliced (optional)

Sea salt and black pepper

You'll need a medium ovenproof dish. I use a round cast-iron pan that's got a bit of depth to it. Grease the dish or pan with the butter and make sure you hit the sides so the pie doesn't stick to the pan.

Chuck the cheese, onion and mayonnaise into a large bowl. Add a glug of Worcestershire sauce, the oregano and a pinch of salt and pepper. Take your magic spoon wand and conjure up greatness (mix well).

Cover the base of the pan with half of the bread cubes. You only want one layer, as there's another to go. Next, cover the bread with a layer of sliced tomatoes (saving your best-looking slices for later), slightly overlapping. Season with salt and pepper. Then throw on another layer of bread.

It's cheesy time! Using a spatula, cover the bread with half the cheese mix. Now use your school art skills to make a perfect layer of your best tomato slices overlapping gorgeously on top of the cheese mix. Then slather the rest of the cheese mix on top of the tomatoes. Finally, make it rain with spring onion and red chilli slices, and crack a bit more pepper on top.

Make sure your cooker is at around 190°C (375°F). For more help on this, see Controlling the Heat on page 12.

Place the pie over the heat canyon on the indirect heat. Place the lid on and cook for 25–30 minutes – the lid will help it turn golden on top.

SCALLOPS WITH GRILLED PINEAPPLE AND CHORIZO

The inspiration for this recipe came from my yearly trips to the Isle of Man off the west coast of England. This tiny island hosts one of the most dangerous motorbike races in the world, the Isle of Man TT. It is the gnarliest thing I have ever witnessed. Apart from motorbike racing, the island is famous for scallops, especially 'queenies', which are smaller than your classic scallop. I pretty much eat scallops every day when I go there. Twice a day if queenies are in season! This recipe is almost like a Hawaiian pizza but with fish and no bread or cheese. Come to think of it, this is nothing like a Hawaiian pizza. Move on Stevenson... tell 'em how to make this awesomely simple dish.

🍴 SERVES 2-3

🍖 BBQ SET-UP
Half and half technique

½ pineapple, cored and cut into 1cm (½ inch) slices

100g (3½oz) chorizo, cut into chunks

12 small to medium scallops, cleaned. I like to keep the roe (coral bit)

Knob of butter

2 spring onions (scallions), sliced

Juice of ½ lemon

Black pepper

This bad boy can go from prep to serve in 15 minutes.

Grill the pineapple slices until you have a lovely char. This will take a bit longer than you think, because of the water content of the pineapple. But don't be lazy, get those suckers off as soon as you have the char marks on both sides. Place the grilled slices onto a chopping board and cut into chunks.

At this point, check your cooker is still good and hot. You'll need to get a hot heat rocking to achieve a char on the scallops. If things get out of hand you can use the indirect side, which you might need while cooking the chorizo.

Place a large cast-iron frying pan (skillet) over direct heat. When the pan is hot, chuck in the chorizo and render down that glorious fat. Once you see the orange liquid in the pan, remove the chorizo but keep the oils in the pan for the scallops. Do not let the chorizo burn. Move the pan towards the middle or indirect side to calm things down if you need to.

Put the pan back on the direct heat and get her rocking! Hot hot! When the pan starts to smoke, chuck your scallops in. Get that all-important sear happening. It's the most essential thing when cooking scallops. After 30–60 seconds, give them a flip and get that dollop of butter straight into the pan. Baste the scallops with the melted butter, using a large spoon, until they are just cooked, another 30 seconds or so. Now add the grilled pineapple chunks, chorizo, spring onions and lemon juice. Toss and serve with a dusting of cracked pepper. Yup, one of the best things you'll ever cook. Congratulations.

MISO STEAK KEBABS

This recipe screams 'Yummy!' from the get-go! Plus, it's very versatile. You can put loads of different ingredients on the skewer. Perfect when you need to clear out the fridge. All you need is a lead singer – and today's Mick Jagger is the almighty ribeye steak. Other cuts of meat are available, but I would always recommend a good fatty, thick grilling steak.

✎ **SERVES 4**

🍖 **BBQ SET-UP**
Half and half technique. You will also need metal skewers or soaked wood skewers

100g (3½oz) miso paste

2 x 300g (10½oz) thick ribeye steaks or classic grilling steaks, sliced into large chunks

2 red onions, peeled and quartered

1 aubergine (eggplant), chopped into chunks

2 pears, cored and quartered

12 chestnut mushrooms

1 courgette (zucchini), chopped into chunks

2 red/green/yellow (bell) peppers, chopped into 4cm (1½-inch) squares

Olive oil

Sea salt and black pepper

For the spice blend

1 tbsp salt

½ tbsp cracked pepper

½ tbsp onion granules

½ tbsp garlic granules

1 tbsp paprika

1 tsp dried thyme

Olive oil

There are two ways of rocking this recipe. One will be tasty as hell. And the other will be almost as good. Basically, you can either marinate overnight or brush the marinade on while cooking. I do it both ways, and both ways are awesome. But the overnight marinade is just that little bit better, as the miso flavours are more in your face. So, for the more intense flavour, rub the miso paste all over your steak chunks and leave to marinate overnight or for at least a couple of hours.

The next day, mix up your rub for the veggies in a bowl. You can double the quantity and transfer half to an airtight container so you can easily break out this epic rub on your next cookout.

Once your veggies are chopped up, place them in a large bowl, drizzle with a glug of olive oil then make it rain spice blend! Mix thoroughly so all the veggies have lapped up the olive oil and flavours.

When you're ready to cook, slide your meat and veg onto the skewers. Before you get crazy with the rainbow of ingredients, think steak, red onion and pear! Put these three together, as it's the perfect combination of flavours.

Get your skewers on the direct heat. If you haven't pre-marinated the steak, then brush the steak with the miso paste once it's started to colour. Turn the skewers during the cook so all sides of the kebab have a good colour and caramelization. Finish off the cook on the indirect side, until your meat is blushing and the veg and fruit are golden.

Pull 'em off the grill, and serve! The best kebabs you will ever cook in your entire existence on this planet and it's super-duper triply easy to do. Well done! You rule! Now go order tickets for the Van Halen reunion tour and sing 'Panama' as loud as humanly possible.

PICANHA

★ ★

Picanha is awesome! My love for it was sealed when I went on a road trip around the south of Brazil with the food critic Giles Coren, to visit the pampas (grassland) and cattle farms where they raise some of the best cows on the planet. I was very fortunate to go cattle herding on two of the most renowned farms on the border of Uruguay in the Baja area. I herded pure Black Angus, which are world famous. We went to a local restaurant and just had to order the picanha – Brazil's most popular cut of beef for grilling. I spent time with a good friend from Brazil called Andre Lima de Luca. He's cooked the most exquisite picanha I've had the pleasure of tasting. I learned how to cook picanha from Andre and taken this awesome Brazilian cut of meat and given it a bit of my adopted Englishness. In London, they've been roasting beef with a coating of English mustard powder for over 100 years. Couple this with a little earthy nutmeg and she is a force to be reckoned with. Just wait till you cut the first steaks!

🔪 SERVES 6-8

🍖 BBQ SET-UP
Half and half technique

1 large picanha (rump cap with fat) (about 1–1.5kg/2lb 4oz–3lb 5oz), at room temperature

Sea salt and black pepper

For the rub

2 tbsp sea salt

1 tbsp black pepper

2 tbsp yellow mustard powder

1 tsp ground nutmeg

First, take that big old cut of beef out of the fridge and let it relax and get to room temperature. In the meantime, make your rub by mixing the salt, pepper, mustard powder and nutmeg in a small bowl. Get your cooker rocking a good medium hot heat.

Score the fat on your beef and dry it with kitchen (paper) towel. Then rub in the spice mix, making sure you get it into all the score lines. Rub the beef all over, so the meat is evenly covered, but be careful not to rub too much, so the spices clump together. It should look like a nice thick dusting. Now give the rub some time to dry out the fat slightly, about 5–10 minutes. Fat is made up of a lot of water, so we want to lose some of that moisture so the fat can cook.

First, we need to get that fat cap rendering. We are not cooking the inside yet, just the outside. So place the joint fat side down over direct heat. We are looking for a golden crust all over the meat, and nicely rendered fat. Keep an eye on it – you will get flare-ups as the fats break down. A couple of blasts are ok, but you'll need to move the meat around so it's getting a nice even rendering. Keep turning it as well, to sear the meat properly all over and build up that mustardy crust.

Recipe continues...

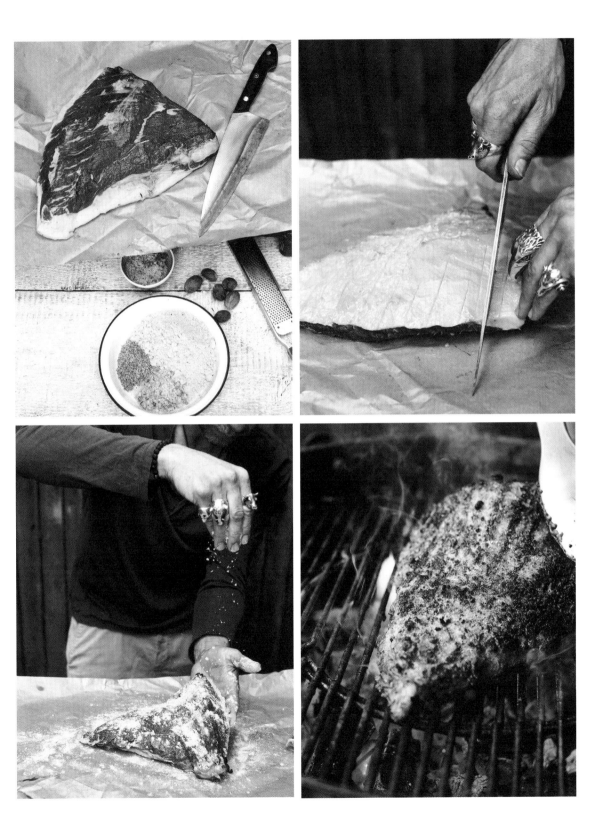

Recipe continued from p118

It's all about movement. Make sure you pay attention to the rump's fat cap and get it cooking but don't burn it. Fat is flavour and we need to get that fat working.

Once you have that lovely crust, but the inside is still raw, take it off the heat and let it rest for 10 minutes. Once it has rested, slice the joint into 2.5cm (1-inch) steaks along the grain. The colour is quite amazing – you've got the crimson claret of the meat matched with the rendered golden fat... mmmm, this is making me hungry but it's only gonna get better.

Sprinkle some salt on the steaks and off you go. Grill them like a normal steak over direct heat. I like these medium–rare. Once you've got your steaks to where you want them (see the note on page 102), pull them off and serve up.

To serve up, slice across the grain to show that sweet sweet fat off. Enjoy. Cold beer time!

BEACH BAR GRILLED OCTOPUS

My favourite place in the world to chill and eat is the Beach Bar in Burgau, Portugal. My good friends Adriano and Marco Shepherd own and run this lovely establishment. It's right on the beach and couldn't be more picturesque. I've filmed numerous recipes here and their food has inspired many of my dishes, including this one. These dudes are family. Good luck getting a table here in August though. Last time I went, I just missed out on hanging with Billy Idol who spent an entire week eating and drinking at the Beach Bar. I know Madonna, Metallica, Lionel Ritchie and Ariana Grande told me to quit name-dropping, but Billy Idol is surely worthy of a mention.

🍴 **SERVES 4-6**
tapas-sized portions (octopus can be a bit heavy eating so less is more even though you will defo want seconds and thirds)

🍖 **BBQ SET-UP**
Half and half technique

1kg (2lb 4oz) octopus (frozen or fresh), head removed and gutted, tentacles separated as close to the head as possible

2 tbsp olive oil

1 onion, peeled and halved

4 garlic cloves, peeled and smashed

500ml (17fl oz/generous 2 cups) water

125ml (4¼fl oz/generous ½ cup) white wine

1 red chilli, sliced, to garnish

The key to octopus is tenderizing it before cooking. I've seen kids in Greece whacking them on rocks but I prefer to freeze the octopus overnight. Or buy the octopus already frozen.

First up, make the marinade. Mix all the marinade ingredients in a bowl.

If you want to take this recipe to the next level, buy the octopus fresh, place it in a ziplock bag together with the marinade, then freeze it with the marinade overnight. This will tenderize the octopus and infuse it with even more flavour.

If you are using frozen octopus, allow it to defrost, and place it in a ziplock bag together with the marinade. Leave to marinate overnight in the fridge.

Get a large saucepan with a lid – big enough to fit all the octopus pieces in – and place it over the direct heat. Once hot, add the oil and roast the onion and smashed garlic for 5–6 minutes until golden. Add the water and wine and bring to the boil. (You could do this part in the kitchen, but where's the fun in that?!)

Recipe continues...

For the marinade

2 bay leaves

100ml (3½fl oz/scant ½ cup) extra virgin olive oil

Juice of 1 lemon

5cm (2 inches) ginger, peeled and grated (shredded)

50ml (1¾fl oz/scant ¼ cup) light soy sauce

Pinch of black pepper

Pinch of garlic granules

Pinch of paprika

For the garlic basting sauce

2 tbsp butter

2 tbsp olive oil

4 garlic cloves, peeled and smashed

Cracked black pepper, to taste

Pinch of chilli flakes (optional)

For the rocket (arugula) pesto (optional)

2–3 handfuls of rocket (arugula)

2 tbsp pine nuts

1 garlic clove

4 tbsp olive oil

Sea salt and black pepper

Recipe continued from p122

Add the marinated octopus, move the pan to the indirect heat, and slowly simmer with the lid on for 1½–2 hours. Make sure you only have light bubbles. This is a slow and low cook. Add more water if it starts to dry out.

Check the tenderness of the octopus with a sharp knife in the thickest part of the tentacle. Once tender, remove from the pot and chill in the fridge. This whole process can be done the day before.

When you are ready to eat, get the grill stonking. If you're making the rocket pesto, you can whizz all the ingredients in a blender – you're looking for a paste that's easy to drizzle, so add more rocket or olive oil as necessary. Transfer to a bowl, cover, and place in the fridge to chill.

Once the cooker is hot, place a small saucepan near the direct heat and add all the ingredients for the basting sauce. Leave this to heat gently for 5–10 minutes so the flavours can become best friends. Be careful not to burn this sauce.

Place the octopus tentacles straight on the grill over the direct heat and start basting with the sauce. The octopus is already cooked by this time, so you are mostly looking to get a good char rocking on the tentacles. Grill, turn and baste for 3–5 minutes until you have a nice char and they are heated through.

Garnish with the sliced chilli and serve straightaway, ideally with chips, rocket pesto and a nice glass of vinho verde or cold beer.

THE DIRTY CHAPTER

THERE'S ONLY SO
MUCH REAL ESTATE
ON THE GRILL – TAKE
YOUR FOOD INTO THE
COALS AND EXPLORE
A WHOLE NEW WORLD
OF LIVE FIRE COOKING

DIRTY LOADED
LOBSTER ROLLS

★ ★

Lobster rules. Lobster is the Ferrari of seafood. It's the holy grail. It's what everyone wants to eat. So give the people what they want! It's always a special day when there's lobster on the grill.

🍴 **SERVES 4**

🍖 **BBQ SET-UP**
   Dirty technique

100g (3½oz) salted butter

2 garlic cloves, sliced

1 chilli, sliced

1 tbsp fresh thyme leaves

2 whole raw lobsters (about 600g/1lb 5oz each), humanely killed, halved lengthways

Juice of ½ lemon

To serve

4 burger buns (I prefer brioche as this is quite a decadent meal)

4 tbsp mayonnaise

½ a bunch of chives, snipped

Get a nice bed of coals cooking. Once they've hit core temperature and have started to ash up, then you are good to go.

While this is happening, melt your butter in a small saucepan and add the garlic, chilli and thyme leaves (you can do this in the kitchen or on the grill). Once the butter starts bubbling, take it off the heat. Set it aside.

Now let's cook these things. Blow the ash off the coals, then lay the lobster halves flesh side down on the coals for 1–2 minutes depending on the size of your lobster. Once you have a nice char, gently turn them over and brush with the flavoured butter. Oh my gosh, I want to eat this right now. Cook for another couple of minutes shell side down, brushing every 30 seconds. The meat will pull away from the shell when it's cooked and it's time to take 'em off.

Leave them to rest for a couple of minutes on a metal tray and pop your butter back on the grill to keep warm.

Gently remove the flesh from the tails and claws. Brush again with the butter. Finish with the lemon juice.

Toast your buns. Spread a dollop of mayo on the base of the toasted bun. Pile the lobster meat high and sprinkle on the chives.

By the way, you just won the game of life with this cookout. I'm off to the fishmonger to buy some more lobster.

DIRTY OYSTER TACO

Oysters are built to be cooked on coals – they provide their own frying pan and cooking liquid, which is RAD! This recipe is everything I love about grilling on a beach. You just need a bed of coals, some really basic equipment and a few ingredients. Damn, these are good!

🍴 **SERVES 4**

🍖 **BBQ SET-UP**
Dirty technique

12 oysters, opened and the meat loosened
8 soft tortilla wraps

For the paprika butter

1 tsp paprika
4 garlic cloves, peeled and crushed
Small bunch of coriander (cilantro), stems finely chopped (keep the leaves for the salsa)
50g (1¾oz) butter, softened
Juice of 1 lemon

For the grapefruit salsa

1 pink grapefruit, peeled and segmented
½ red onion, finely chopped
Juice of 1 lime
Small bunch of coriander (cilantro), leaves chopped
1 jalapeño chilli, finely chopped

For the chipotle sour cream
300ml (10½fl oz/1¼ cups) sour cream
2 tbsp chipotle chilli paste

Find a nice quiet place on the beach. You don't want a lot of wind. Dig a small pit and get a nice bed of coals rockin' and ready for dirty cooking.

While your fire is cooking down, go for a quick shred on those awesome afternoon sets that are coming in. Then get the rest of the food prepped up.

First, make the paprika butter by mixing all the ingredients together with a fork. Set aside.

For the salsa, quickly grill the grapefruit segments on the coals. You need to be really quick as you only want a very slight char on them. Chop them up, put them in a bowl with the rest of the salsa ingredients, give it a good mix and set it aside.

Make the chipotle sour cream by mixing the sour cream and chilli paste together. You can add a little less of the chilli paste if you don't want it too hot.

When you are ready to cook, spoon a dollop of paprika butter on each opened oyster and get them straight on the bed of coals. The butter will melt quickly and cook the oysters. Once the butter is bubbling, cook for 3 or 4 minutes, using a small spoon to baste the oyster meat if it needs it.

Remove the oysters from the heat and set aside to rest while you char your wraps on the grill. Then build your beach tacos there and then, with the oysters, grapefruit salsa and chipotle sour cream.

Enjoy these puppies while watching the sun drop!

DIRTY ONIONS

Onions are sometimes clean, other times they are dirty. I like 'em dirty. It's a bit like being in a club at 9.30am on a Monday morning when you know the owner is not happy you're wearing a charcoal-encrusted cat suit with a small goat in tow. But you are only there because they do steak and eggs for £4.99 with a beer. You can't beat a deal like that. Whenever we have a cookout, we begin with getting some big old onions into the coals. During the festival season, we cook 30kg (66lb) of onions a day and always dirty! Dirty onions are a great foundation for so many dishes. There's three flavour profiles you'll find when using this cooking technique: 1) smoky onion ash flavour from the outer layer; 2) slow-roasted caramelized flavour from the middle layer; 3) sweet and tangy flavour from the centre. How ya like them apples... I mean onions?

⚱ BBQ SET-UP
Dirty technique

Onions (the larger the better – I use huge Spanish ones)

Make sure your coals have properly cooked down and are not too fierce. The coal bed should be evenly laid out.

Whatever you do, do not peel the onions. You need the outer casing to protect the sweet tangy flesh within. Once the coals are good to go, take a pair of tongs and carefully place the onions straight into the coals. Push the coals around the onions so that they get hit from all sides. You don't need to cover the onions as you'll turn them a couple of times during the cook. The big ones should take anywhere from 1½ hours to 2 hours. The perfect dirty onion will 'pop' from the top. This is when the centre gets hotter than the sun and erupts like a volcano. Be careful of the lava. Not every onion will pop but the majority do. To make sure the onions are done, give them a squeeze with the tongs. They should be really quite soft. Be careful not to overcook them, as once the moisture has been cooked out, they will go hard as a rock, especially if they are small ones.

Carefully take the onions out of the coals and rest them on a baking tray (sheet) covered with foil. This helps the onions rehydrate. Be careful in case there are any coals, which can sometimes stick to the onions. You can use them right away but they are pretty hot. We normally cook onions in the morning and let them cool down for a couple of hours before handling.

The best technique for getting into the goodness is to squeeze the skin and pop the onion out. Remove the ash and dried skin but don't worry if little bits of charred skin remain – they only add flavour and texture. These can now be chopped and used in a variety of recipes or as a condiment. Soak them in a little bit of cider vinegar and a pinch of salt for next-level flavour.

DIRTY CARROTS WITH MAPLE SYRUP AND CUMIN

Veggies love live fire just as much as meat. I know I bang on about dirty onions (see p134) all the time, but they are such a staple in my cooking. So are these sweet and tasty charred carrots cooked dirty style. This is one of the easiest recipes to cook up when going dirty. Plus, you save room on the top-floor grill. I love using the coal bed for nailing lovely smoky char flavour on the veg.

 SERVES 3–4
as a side dish

BBQ SET-UP
Dirty technique

12 large carrots, washed, not peeled

4 tbsp maple syrup

2 tbsp balsamic vinegar

1 tbsp cumin seeds

Sea salt and black pepper

Get a nice coal bed cooked up and, once the coals start to ash, you are good to go. Place your carrots straight into the coals. Use a pair of tongs to snuggle the coals around the carrots so more surface area is being cooked by the coals.

Turn the carrots every 5 minutes to stop them from charring too much. After about 20–25 minutes, the carrots should be cooked – they should bend nicely but not be floppy. Once you have the bend, remove the carrots from the coals and place on a metal tray. Let them cool down before moving onto the next step as they will be too hot to handle.

Slice the carrots on the angle and lay them back in the tray. Drizzle the maple syrup and balsamic vinegar over the carrots and mix things up. Make it rain cumin seeds, flakes of salt and freshly ground pepper, and give the tray a lovely shake so all the carrots are seasoned.

Place the tray on top of the coals to caramelize the syrup. Keep stirring the carrots until the syrup starts to bubble, then remove and enjoy one of life's tastiest side dishes. Or this could be part of a main event for my veggie and vegan friends.

BABAGANOUSH

This recipe was inspired by my university days in Maryland. I used to study bowling – yes it was actually a course worth two credits. Next to the bowling alley was the school co-op where students could work off their lunch. It was a proper hippy joint and it was where I first had hummus and babaganoush. I liked to party at university so my babaganoush, hummus and shredded carrot sandwich was my attempt to heal my broken body. It wasn't all bad, as I made it to the finals of my Intermediate Bowling course – where I lost. Speaking of bowling, they call me 'The Janitor' because I always clean up my frames with a strike or spare. I once bowled a 230 with six strikes in a row on the island of Sareema, off the west coast of Estonia. My life is complete due to that fabulous feat – and this recipe. You can also mix the babaganoush with mayo to make an amazing mayonnaise for your burger.

✎ **SERVES 6**
as a side

 BBQ SET-UP
Dirty technique

2 large aubergines (eggplants)

1 garlic bulb

Juice of ½ lemon

2 tbsp tahini

1 tbsp extra virgin olive oil

Sea salt and black pepper

Place the aubergines straight onto the coals and sit the garlic bulb right next to them to hot-roast.

After about 20–30 minutes your aubergines will be as soft as butter. Pull them out of the coals onto a metal tray, cover with foil and leave to rest for another 30 minutes, so they don't lose any more moisture. Check the garlic to see if it's tender and soft. If it is, remove and let it cool with the aubergines.

Slice down the middle of the aubergine and scoop out the smoky flesh onto a board. Don't worry if you end up with some charred bits in the mix – this will only add lovely flavour and look cool.

Peel and squeeze out the roasted garlic flesh. Add this to the aubergine flesh, along with the lemon juice, tahini and olive oil and season with salt and pepper. Using a large cook's knife, finely chop and pulp the ingredients together, until you get a chunky paste.

Use the side of the knife to crush the paste until smooth and truly awesome.

Throw it all in a bowl and serve it up with some lamb, like the Next-level Lamb Wrap on page 54.

CIDER VINEGAR INFUSED WITH CHARCOAL

Cider vinegar is one of the most integral ingredients when cooking BBQ. And it's pretty easy to make. It gives a wonderful tangy flavour to your food and, if it contains the 'mother', vinegar has incredible health benefits. It's really good for digestion, which helps when eating so much delicious BBQ. People say it can lower blood pressure, help with losing weight and help manage diabetes. And, it's easier to make than actual real cider (hard cider) as you just leave the freshly fermented cider in a cupboard and let the air get to it. If you are making either one of these concoctions, you might as well make both. The only ingredient is apples, any variety, but preferably ones from your garden. These are best as they won't have any pesticides and will be covered in loads of natural yeast.

✎ MAKES 1 LARGE JAR

🍴 BBQ SET-UP
Dirty technique

3kg (6¾lb) fresh, untreated apple, see introduction

Large fermenting tub

Lid with bubbler cork

Organic (untreated) apple wood chunks

Get your apples and crush them into a big clean container. This can be done with a cheese grater (shredder), apple pulper or a fence post (preferably a clean one). Take a big handful of the pulp and place it in a clean tea towel over a large bowl. Bring the edges together and twist them to make a tight parcel. Keep twisting to extract all the juice, catching it in the bowl. Discard the pulp when it is dry and keep going until you have used up all your pulp.

Pour the juice into the fermenting tub, leaving a small air gap, and seal the lid with a bubbler cork installed. Leave to ferment for 3–4 weeks at room temperature. This will create all that oh so lovely alcohol, but – for the first time in the history of you – you don't want this alcohol. We are going to turn it into acetic acid. This acid is what makes our cider vinegar so tangy and such a useful ingredient.

To achieve this, all you need to do is let the air get to the cider. This means the acetic acid bacteria can convert the ethanol to acetic acid. Once the apple juice has fermented into cider, open the lid and cover the tub with a single piece of cheesecloth, secured with a piece of string. Leave it for another 3–4 weeks, stirring every few days.

Recipe continues...

Recipe continued from p142

So, after a couple of months, you have an awesome vinegar that took less time to make than walking from John o' Groats to Land's End! Easy. Now to next level the shit out of this donkey kong of ingredients.

First, you need to make some fresh charcoal made out of some untreated apple wood – don't use wood from a tree that gets treated with pesticides and other chemicals. Light a small fire with any wood/charcoal and place some chunks of your apple wood in a tin (such as an old biscuit tin or tea tin) with a small hole in the lid. Place the tin on the fire and cook until you stop seeing smoke (this might take a few hours). When you stop seeing smoke, remove the tin from the fire and turn it upside down to cover the hole. Leave to cool for a couple of hours. It's important not to let the air get to the coals or they will combust if still hot. Once cool, remove the coals from the tin and keep until you want to use them.

When you are ready to infuse the cider vinegar you have so gloriously made, put it in a stainless-steel bowl or saucepan. Light a small fire and get a couple of chunks of that apple charcoal burning. Leave them a few moments to fully ignite, then use a pair of tongs to drop them carefully into the cider. This will make the cider vinegar bubble and infuse it with smoky apple flavour. Leave for half an hour, then strain the vinegar through cheesecloth into a sterilized bottle.

The vinegar will keep for a couple of months but it won't last that long in my house. You can use it as a seasoning for any meat, or make a BBQ sauce with it. Or just drink the stuff. I like to have a swig every morning to get my gut balanced for the day. You can use it in any recipe in this book that calls for cider vinegar (of which there are many!).

SIDE SHOWS

ALL THE MAIN EVENTS IN
THIS BOOK NEED SOME
SUPPORT! OR YOU
CAN SUPERSIZE THESE
DISHES AND MAKE
THEM THE STARS

SMOKED POTATO SALAD

BBQ and potato salad go hand in hand but me and the crew changed the game by adding sweet smoky flavours to this classic. When we created this dish, it quickly became our friends' favourite complement to a meaty cookout. In fact, many of our friends have said that this is their all-time favourite dish of all our tasty treats. Yup, it's that good.

✎ **SERVES 6**
as a side

🍖 **BBQ SET-UP**
Half and half technique. Seasoned wood chunks

1kg (2lb 4oz) potatoes (good-quality waxy ones like Charlotte or new potatoes), halved

2 tbsp olive oil

Small bunch of coriander (cilantro)

4 tbsp mayonnaise

4 spring onions (scallions), chopped

2 red chillies, sliced

Juice of 1 lemon

Sea salt and black pepper

Get your cooker to around 220°C (430°F). This is a proper hot smoke! For more help on this, see Controlling the Heat on page 12.

Put a large saucepan of water on to boil on the direct side of the grill. Once boiling, par-boil your potatoes for 10 minutes.

Drain the spuds and let them dry in a colander for at least 15 minutes. The longer the better.

When dry, throw your potatoes into a large bowl and rub with olive oil and a pinch of salt and pepper.

Tip the potatoes onto the indirect side of the grill. Throw some wood chunks into your coals and put the lid on. Cook for 40–60 minutes until you have a smoky golden colour on the skin of the spuds. Keep an eye on the temperature and make sure you don't burn the spuds.

Remove the smoky potatoes from the cooker and let them rest. You can serve this dish warm or cold, so it's up to you how long you leave them. Meanwhile, pick the coriander leaves but don't throw away the stems (we love them, they have great flavour). Roughly chop the leaves and finely chop the stems.

In a large bowl, mix the smoked spuds with the mayo, spring onions, sliced chillies, lemon juice and coriander leaves and stems. Serve with something massive! Like a spatchcock chicken (see p94).

WHOLE HARISSA ROASTED CAULIFLOWER

Cauliflowers are like badgers, they live underground and make good hats! Confused? Well if I can't catertain you, I'll at least confuse you! But seriously, this recipe is anything but confusing. It makes a tasty main event or side dish and is great for your vegetarian friends.

SERVES 6
as a side

 BBQ SET-UP
Heat canyon technique.
Seasoned wood chunks

1 large cauliflower

100ml harissa paste (shop-bought or home-made, see below)

Juice of 1 lemon

Handful of fresh mint leaves, chopped

Sea salt and black pepper

For the harissa paste

8–10 red chillies

2 chipotle chillies

1 tbsp chilli flakes (isot pul biber flakes are the best)

1 tsp ground cumin

1 tsp ground caraway seeds

1 tsp ground coriander

2 garlic cloves, peeled

1 tbsp dark brown sugar

1 tbsp vinegar

1 tsp sea salt

2–3 tbsp olive oil

First, we need to make the harissa paste. Blitz all the paste ingredients in a blender. Boom! You made harissa paste. Or be lazy and go buy a jar or can of the stuff.

Get your outdoor cooker to 150–160°C (300–320°F). Add your seasoned wood chunks to the coals. For more help on this, see Controlling the Heat on page 12.

Put a large saucepan of water on the direct heat and bring to a boil. Par-boil the cauliflower head for 4–5 minutes. Drain and place the cauliflower on a chopping board. Use a spatula to slather the head with the harissa paste. Go heavy for full-on spiciness or lightly for just a hint of a kick.

Place the cauliflower over the heat canyon on the indirect heat, and put the lid on the cooker. Hot roast for 45–60 minutes until the cauliflower goes dark red and tender.

When it's done, pull it off and slice into 2.5cm (1-inch) thick steaks. Squeeze lemon juice all over, season and finish with the chopped mint.

RUBY'S GREEN BEAN CASSEROLE

If I wasn't in the backyard cooking out with Dad, then I was in the kitchen with Mom learning to bake and do all sorts of indoor recipes. Momma (Ruby) would roll this dish out every holiday and for Sunday roasts. This is my favourite side dish to go with a roast turkey. It's super-easy to make and so delicious.

✎ **SERVES 4**

♨ **BBQ SET-UP**
   Heat canyon technique

1kg (2lb 4oz) green beans, trimmed

1 x 400g (14oz) can cream of mushroom soup

125ml (4½fl oz/generous ½ cup) whole milk

1 tsp nutmeg

1 tsp smoked paprika

Crispy onions (you can buy these ready-fried in most supermarkets, or you can fry your own)

Sea salt and black pepper

Bring a saucepan of water to boil on the direct heat and blanch the beans for 2 minutes. Drain and cool in cold water to stop them going brown.

Lay the beans in an ovenproof dish. Stir in the can of soup and the milk. Then add the spices, and season with salt and pepper. Mix well and place over the heat canyon on the indirect heat for 20–25 minutes. Make sure your lid is on the cooker as you need to keep the heat in.

Sprinkle crispy onions onto the beans and cook for an additional 5 minutes with the lid on. Take the dish off the grill and serve. Make sure there's a big old roasted turkey to go along with these bad-ass beans.

BAKING THE LAW!
BAKING THE LAW!
BAKED BEANS

★ ★

Every good pitmaster, backyard chef and amateur cook needs to have a good recipe for baked beans in their repertoire. And because you so kindly asked, here's a super duper triply delicious one for your viewing and eating pleasure. So good, you gotta break a few laws to make it. First up, the law of mediocre flavours.

🍴 SERVES 6-8

🍖 BBQ SET-UP
Heat canyon technique. Seasoned wood chunks

200g (7oz) bacon lardons (fatty bacon, cubed)

1 red chilli (or go with however many you can handle... break the law!)

2 red onions, sliced

2 carrots, peeled and sliced

1 leek, sliced

1 garlic bulb, whole cloves peeled and smashed

1 tsp paprika

1 tsp ground coriander

1 tsp sumac

1 cinnamon stick

Ingredients continue overleaf

You'll need a roasting tin (pan) that will fit on the grill.

Put your bacon in the tin and try to get them fat side down. Place on your grill over the heat canyon on the indirect heat. Stick your chillies straight on the grill over the indirect heat to char, then put the lid on. After 20 minutes, the bacon fat will have rendered and the chillies will be smoky and roasted.

Add all the roasted veg and the spices (up to and including the cinnamon stick) to the tin, give the whole lot a good mix and get it back on the grill with the lid on for another 30 minutes, stirring well halfway through.

When the veggies are starting to char, add in all the rest of the ingredients, up to and including the parsley stems (but not the leaves) and place back on the grill with the lid on, for another 45 minutes.

After 45 minutes, pull those suckers off and give them a big old stir! If these break your heart and probably a couple of laws, then you know you're one step closer to bringing around world peace.

Finish these bad boys off by stirring in the balsamic vinegar and season with a little salt and pepper if needed. Then make it rain chopped parsley leaves.

50ml (1¾fl oz/scant ¼ cup) bourbon

500ml (17fl oz/generous 2 cups) passata

200ml (7fl oz/generous ¾ cup) BBQ sauce (I recommend T-Bone's BBQ Sauce, see p175)

3 x 400g (14oz) cans beans, drained

Handful of rosemary leaves, chopped

Handful of thyme leaves, chopped

Handful of sage leaves, chopped

2 chipotle chillies

2 parsley sprigs, stems chopped (leaves reserved to garnish)

2 tbsp balsamic vinegar

Sea salt and black pepper

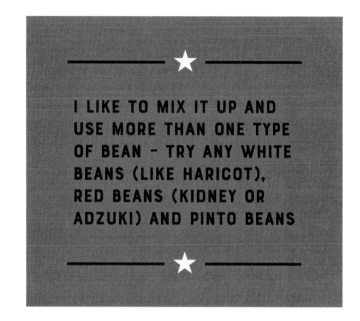

I LIKE TO MIX IT UP AND USE MORE THAN ONE TYPE OF BEAN - TRY ANY WHITE BEANS (LIKE HARICOT), RED BEANS (KIDNEY OR ADZUKI) AND PINTO BEANS

GRILLED OKRA

I discovered okra on a 1990 road trip from Maryland on the east coast to San Diego, California. I was driving a 1986 Black Ford Ranger with my friend Michael Sowinski (who we had renamed Michael 'So Stinky'). We were travelling through some desolate roads in Oklahoma and had to stop to refuel the truck and our bodies. This is where I had deep-fried okra. And for years, I only had it this way until I tried grilling it. I wanted to achieve the same consistency as the classic grilled padrón peppers but without the okra going slimy, which it can do. This is a super-simple and easy recipe. And makes a good starter or side dish to any cookout.

 SERVES 4-6
as a side

BBQ SET-UP
Half and half technique

500g (1lb 2oz) okra

2 tbsp olive oil

1 tsp cayenne pepper

Sea salt and black pepper

Juice of 1 lemon, to serve

For the topping

50ml (1¾fl oz/scant ¼ cup) vegetable oil

4 garlic cloves, sliced

1 red chilli, deseeded and thinly sliced

1 tbsp cumin seeds

Place your okra in a deep tray or bowl. Drizzle with the olive oil, sprinkle with the cayenne pepper and season with salt and pepper. Mix everything together so that the okra is evenly coated.

Now make the topping. Line a metal baking tray (sheet) with kitchen (paper) towel. Heat the vegetable oil in a small saucepan over the direct heat. Once hot, add the garlic, chilli, cumin and a pinch of salt. Fry until the garlic turns golden, then drain everything on the kitchen towel.

Now get your okra onto the direct heat. Grill, turning, until soft, charred and tender.

Once the okra is good to go, take it off the grill and put it in a serving bowl. Top with the garlic-chilli-cumin topping. Finish with the lemon juice.

This goes killer with lamb. My god, how did you make okra so ding dong dang tasty? Congrats to you and your grilling prowess. Veggies love live fire!

STUFFED RAINBOW PEPPERS

A couple of years ago, I collaborated with The Happy Pear brothers for a YouTube video. These dudes write some of the best vegetarian cookbooks on earth. We got together and came up with a tasty recipe, then I went away and tweaked it a little. And now it's yours for the making and eating. This could be a main event, or a wonderful side dish, or even a starter.

✎ **SERVES 6**

🍖 **BBQ SET-UP**
Half and half technique

2 red dirty onions (see p134)

150g (5½oz/¾ cup) couscous

200ml (7fl oz/generous ¾ cup) cold water

2 red (bell) peppers

2 green (bell) peppers

2 yellow (bell) peppers

50g (1¾oz/scant ½ cup) flaked (slivered) almonds

50g (1¾oz/generous ¾ cup) pistachios

1 courgette (zucchini), sliced lengthways

1 cucumber, peeled and sliced lengthways

Bunch of asparagus

1 red and 1 green chilli

Olive oil, for drizzling

Juice of 1 lemon

200g (7oz) feta, in chunks

Sea salt and black pepper

Get your onions cooking in the coals (see Dirty Onions, p134). Once cooked, set aside to cool, then peel and roughly chop.

Pour the couscous into a small roasting tin (pan) that has a lid. Pour the cold water over the couscous until it's just covered. Pop the lid on and place the tin over indirect heat. Bake for 25–30 minutes, stirring every 5 or 6 minutes, until the water has been absorbed and you have a light and fluffy and smoky couscous. Take off the heat and leave to rest.

Put the whole peppers on the direct heat, turning regularly, until you have a lovely caramelization all round. Don't worry if you get some darker bits on the skin. That's just flavour. Move them to the indirect side to cook through until tender. When they are done, carefully slice off the tops (keep them for presentation when you serve) and remove the seeds inside. Set aside until you are ready to assemble.

Toast the nuts in a small dry frying pan (skillet) over the direct heat, until slightly golden, then set aside.

Drizzle olive oil onto the rest of your veg and chillies and get them on the grill. Once they've got a decent char, take them off and roughly chop.

You'll need a fairly large cauldron to mix all these tasty treats. Chuck all the chopped vegetables (including the onions and chillies) into the bowl. Drizzle liberally with olive oil. Add in the toasted nuts, couscous, lemon juice and feta, and season to taste. Mix it all together well and stuff your peppers like your life depended on it. Place the tops back on and serve.

GRILLED WATERMELON AND FETA SALAD

I love a salad, especially one with feta! It's like a naughty and nice salad all in one. The best salads have cheese, and this recipe also works with grilled halloumi.

🍴 **SERVES 4-6**

🍖 **BBQ SET-UP**
   Half and half technique

½ watermelon, cut into 2.5cm (1-inch) slices (save the rinds for pickling, see p173)

50g (1¾oz/⅓ cup) pine nuts

200g (7oz) feta cheese, cut into chunks

Small bunch of mint, leaves picked

Small bunch of flat-leaf parsley, leaves picked and roughly chopped

100g (3½oz/¾ cup) pitted black olives

½ red onion, very thinly sliced

Juice of ½ lime

Remove the rind from your watermelon and grill the slices over the direct heat. Once you have some lovely char from the grill on one side, flip over. I usually grill my watermelon for 3–4 minutes a side.

You want to keep most of the moisture in the flesh, but you'll struggle to get a good char until some of the outer moisture has been cooked off. Allow the watermelon to cool, then cut into cubes, removing as many of the seeds as you can.

Toast the pine nuts in a small dry frying pan (skillet) over the direct heat, until golden.

Grab a big old bowl, chuck in all your ingredients and gently toss. There ya go.

BEER CLAMS

I've lived in Portugal for three summers and spend most of my holiday time visiting friends and family in the Algarve. I can honestly say that this is one of my favourite dishes in the whole world. Heck, my kids even love this dish more than they love me. At the age of six, my son went through two platters of these delicious thangs! Oh, make sure you have some bread to mop up the lovely sauce. The Portuguese call this dish clams Bulhão Pato, after a poet who is now more remembered for clams then his writing. Damn, that's gotta suck. But, at least his name is on menus all over the country. I've done my own take on the Portuguese classic. Some restaurants use white wine when cooking this classic. Me, I use beer. It's better! The malty flavour gives the dish another depth of flavour. It makes it even heartier. I live in England, I like hearty food.

✎ **SERVES 3-4**

🔥 **BBQ SET-UP**
   Half and half technique

1kg (2lb 4oz) clams

3 tbsp extra virgin olive oil

10–12 garlic cloves, smashed

150ml (5fl oz/scant ⅔ cup) lager

Small bunch of coriander (cilantro), stems and leaves separated and chopped

Juice of 1 lemon

Sea salt and black pepper

Put the clams in a sink full of water for a couple of hours to purge them of the sand and grit.

Place a large saucepan (that has a lid) over direct heat, then add the olive oil. When it's hot, add the garlic and get it cooking. As soon as the garlic takes on a bit of colour, add the beer and the coriander stems, and season with salt and pepper. Bring to the boil and add the clams. Stick on the lid and give the pan a good shake. When the liquid comes to the boil again, give it another shake and cook until the clams open up, roughly 5–7 minutes.

Pour everything into a serving dish, including the sauce as you'll definitely want to mop it up with some lovely baguette or toasted sourdough. Now make it rain lemon juice, chopped coriander leaves and freshly ground black pepper. Eat, slurp and dip.

BOURBON AND MAPLE-SPIKED GRAVY

★ ★

I'm gonna say it right now – this is the best gravy you'll ever make. It's easy and amazing and the bourbon gives it a sweet, smoky, sour-mash vibe. And it's a great recipe to batch cook.

✎ SERVES LOADS

🍖 BBQ SET-UP
Heat canyon technique

8 chicken wings

2 onions, sliced

2 carrots, sliced

2 celery sticks, sliced

2 thyme sprigs

2 bay leaves

100g (3½oz) bacon lardons (fatty bacon, cubed)

Olive oil, for drizzling

2 tbsp flour

2 litres (4 pints/8½ cups) hot water

Shot of bourbon

2 tbsp maple syrup

1 tbsp red wine vinegar

2 tbsp wholegrain mustard

You'll need a good-sized roasting tin (pan) for all these goodies. Get your cooker to 175–190ºC (350–375ºF). For more help on this, see Controlling the Heat on page 12.

Chuck the chicken wings, all the veg, thyme, bay leaves and bacon lardons into the tray and drizzle olive oil over it all. Place the tin over the indirect heat and roast for an hour, stirring from time to time. You want to get some nice char and soften up the veg. You can put the lid on the cooker to help.

Add the flour and stir until it is fully mixed in. Slowly pour in the hot water, stirring all the time. Move the tin over the direct heat to bring to the boil. Add the bourbon and maple syrup, move the tin to the indirect heat and cook (with the lid on the cooker) for 20–30 minutes until it is reduced by half. If it gets too thick, you can add more water. You want to intensify the gravy by reducing it but you need to keep it a bit loose.

After 30 minutes, use a potato masher to mash all the ingredients up, releasing the wonderful flavours. Those wings are full of flavour. Remember the sweetest meat is next to the bone and that's why we are using chicken wings.

When you have a rich gravy liquid, strain through a large sieve into a large saucepan. Use the back of a wooden spoon to press and release every vital drop of gravy from the concoction. Finish off with the red wine vinegar and mustard to add an earthy tang that will take your gravy to the upper echelons of amazing flavour.

Save some for another day by freezing it. This gravy goes great with chips or you can make that classic Canadian dish, poutine: chips, cheese curds and the best gravy in the world! For the recipe, turn the page! You lucky people.

HANK'S POUTINE

Poutine! Clogging up arteries for decades. Canadians make two things really well: maple syrup and cheesy gravy chips... otherwise known as poutine. This recipe takes the awesomeness of the Bourbon and Maple-spiked gravy (see p168) and turns it up to the point where it will change your life! Good luck – you will need it when all your buddies come over wanting poutine and beer for the rest of the year.

🔪 **SERVES 6-8**

🏆 **BBQ SET-UP**
Half and half technique. You'll also need a deep-fat fryer

6 large baking potatoes

Olive oil

Sea salt

2–3 litres (3½–5¼ pints/ 8⅓–12½ cups) oil, for deep-fat frying

200g (7oz) goat's curd or soft goat's cheese

1 jug of Bourbon and Maple-spiked gravy (see p168)

Hank the polar bear jug

Get your cooker going at 180°C/350°F. For more help on this, see Controlling the Heat on page 12. To keep a constant temperature for the duration of the cook, you might need to top up your fuel mid-cook. For the best way to top up the fuel, see page 16.

Rub your spuds in olive oil and sea salt and place them over indirect heat on the grill. Put the lid on and cook for 1½–2 hours until cooked through and golden brown. This will dry those suckers out, so you make the best chips since sliced bread, although I do think chips are better than sliced bread in any situation.

When the spuds are cooked, remove them and leave them to cool for at least an hour. This will let them dry out further and make them crisp up! Set your deep-fat fryer to 190°C/370°F.

Cut your cooked spuds into wedges, skin and all! Deep-fry the wedges in batches, draining on kitchen (paper) towel. Fry the wedges until they go beautifully crisp and golden.

When they are all done, lay the cooked wedges out in an oven dish, cover with chunks of the goat's curd and place in the middle of the table. Heat up your gravy until nice and hot and pour it into Hank (the polar bear jug).

When all your buddies are sat down enjoying your favourite Rush track, pour Hank's gravy all over the wedges and curd, so it melts right before their eyes. Now go make some more, 'cos they won't last long!

PICKLED WATERMELON RINDS

Grandma Stevenson was a good gardener – like, really good – so she always had a bountiful harvest. She would pickle almost everything. Her house held myriad pickle jars on every shelf. I ate pickles every day, which is probably where my love of them comes from.

MAKES 2 LARGE JARS

500g (1lb 2oz) watermelon rinds

400ml (14fl oz/1⅔ cups) cider vinegar

300ml (10½fl oz/1¼ cups) water

300g (10½oz/1½ cups) dark brown sugar

1 chilli, halved lengthways

2 tsp coriander seeds

1 tsp black peppercorns

1 tsp whole cloves

1 cinnamon stick, broken into pieces

You will also need 2 sterilized jars and lids

First, make sure you have no remaining flesh on your watermelon rinds, and remove the green skin with a peeler. Chop the white rinds into chunks.

Put the watermelon rinds in a very large saucepan and cover with cold water. Bring the water to the boil and cook the rinds until they go translucent. It takes around 10 minutes, but keep an eye on them – you don't want to overcook them, as they'll go squishy. Drain and place in the warmed sterilized jars.

In another saucepan, bring the rest of the ingredients to a boil. Stir and simmer until the sugar is dissolved. Remove from the heat and pour over the watermelon while hot. Leave to cool down, then screw on the sterilized lids and leave for at least 2 weeks.

QUICK PICKLE

Sometimes you want a pickle, but don't want to wait for it to do its pickling thing. So, I've sorted you out with a quick pickle recipe for when your food needs a nice tangy flavour, fast! This rules! You are welcome.

🍴 MAKES 1 JAR

1 tsp black peppercorns

1 tbsp cumin seeds

1 tbsp chilli flakes

250ml (9fl oz/generous 1 cup) cider vinegar

200ml (7fl oz/generous ¾ cup) water

200g (7oz/1 cup) dark brown sugar

1 tbsp flaked salt

6 pickling cucumbers, sliced

Add the spices to a large dry saucepan and toast for 1–2 minutes until fragrant. Pour in the cider vinegar, water, sugar and salt. Bring to the boil until the sugar dissolves, stirring occasionally.

Take off the heat, add in the sliced cucumbers and leave for at least 15 minutes. Serve on the most awesome of awesome burgers. Awesome!

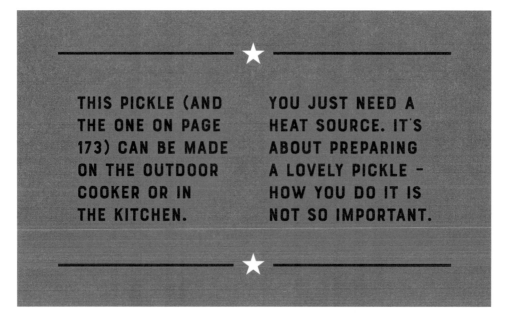

THIS PICKLE (AND THE ONE ON PAGE 173) CAN BE MADE ON THE OUTDOOR COOKER OR IN THE KITCHEN.

YOU JUST NEED A HEAT SOURCE. IT'S ABOUT PREPARING A LOVELY PICKLE – HOW YOU DO IT IS NOT SO IMPORTANT.

T-BONE'S BBQ SAUCE

T-Bone's BBQ sauce is like DJ BBQ sauce but with a hint of Bone and T in it. You could smother an old shoe in this sauce and it will still taste great off the grill... hell, you could even smoke it! Use it with any meat you like. It goes brilliant with bread as well.

✎ SERVES 12

1 dirty onion (see p134)

1 smoked garlic bulb (see p70)

300g (10½oz) fatty pancetta cubes

6 mild red chillies, charred and deseeded with all membrane removed

4 jalapeño chillies, charred and deseeded with all membrane removed

3 sundried tomatoes

1 small can anchovies

2 tbsp capers

6 tbsp tomato paste

Handful of coriander (cilantro) stalks, chopped

½ preserved lemon, chopped

2 tbsp bourbon

6 tbsp dark molasses sugar

1 tbsp sumac

1 tbsp dried juniper berries, crushed

500ml (17fl oz/generous 2 cups) water

1 tbsp honey, plus a little extra if needed

5 tbsp cider vinegar, plus a little extra if needed

Get the onion cooking dirty in the coals. Place the whole bulb of garlic on the grill, and cook for about an hour until smoky and tender (for full instructions, see Dirty Onions on page 134 and Smoked Garlic on page 70). Leave to cool for 30 minutes, peel and chop.

In a deep pan, render down the pancetta cubes for about 20 minutes on a low heat, until you have a good amount of liquid fat. Add in the smoked garlic, dirty onion, chillies, sundried tomatoes, anchovies and capers. (Now you may think: 'anchovies in a bbq sauce?' Well... let me tell you... it's salty, like your mum!)

Fry in the bacon fat for 10 minutes on a low heat until soft and caramelized. Add in the tomato paste, coriander, preserved lemon, bourbon, molasses sugar, sumac and crushed juniper, and cook for 5 minutes until it's starting to reduce.

Add in the water, honey and cider vinegar, and stare at that bubbling cauldron of dark smoky fantasticular brilliance for at least half an hour while it slowly reduces down over a nice gentle heat. Then leave it to cool.

This sauce is totally awesome chunky but if you blend it until smooth, it brings out a much more intense smack in the mouth. It's your choice, hippy...

GREEN SLAW

Every good pitmaster needs a reliable slaw recipe to go with their BBQ. This one will win over even your most sceptical friends.

🍴 SERVES 4-6

150ml (5fl oz/scant ⅔ cup) mayonnaise

2 tbsp cider vinegar

¼ white cabbage, thinly sliced

1 broccoli head, stems thinly sliced, tops reserved for garnish

2 green pears, cored and thinly sliced lengthways

½ fennel bulb, thinly sliced

200g (7oz) sugar snap peas, thinly sliced

4 spring onions (scallions), thinly sliced

Handful of coriander (cilantro), stems finely chopped, leaves reserved for garnish

1 jalapeño chilli, deseeded and thinly sliced

Sea salt and black pepper

This green slaw can be served in two parts: you can keep the crispy fresh salad separate to the mayo; or you can bring it altogether in a creamy slaw spectacular. If keeping it separate, mix the mayo and vinegar together and set aside. Combine all the other ingredients in a bowl.

Otherwise, combine all the ingredients into a large mixing bowl and bring together in the most awesome-tasting moshpit in the history of slaw.

Then chop the reserved coriander leaves and shave the reserved broccoli tops, and garnish.

Serve with your fave BBQ. This goes killer with pulled pork (see p44).

TOMATILLO SALSA

This is my favourite salsa ever. Three summers ago, I was on a journey to find the best taco in California. I shot a bunch of videos for my YouTube channel and got the chance to cook with Conrad Gonzales from Valle Fresh. This incredible chef took me under his wing and showed me the way. When doing this recipe at home, use whatever chillies you can get hold of. Conrad used a whole array of local chillies for his version. But you can keep it quite mellow or go crazy and add a load more. It's really your call.

🔪 SERVES 8-10

🍖 BBQ SET-UP
Half and half technique

10 ripe tomatillos (if you can't find these in a specialist food store, you can buy them online)

1 large white onion, peeled and halved

4 garlic cloves, peeled

1 red chilli

1 green chilli

1 jalapeño or scotch bonnet chilli (use whatever you can get)

Bunch of coriander (cilantro), leaves chopped

Juice of 2 limes

2 tbsp pickle juice (from your own homemade pickle or any jar of pickles)

Pinch of ancho chilli powder

Sea salt and black pepper

Get a large saucepan of water boiling over the direct heat. Add the tomatillos, onion and garlic to the water and boil for about 5 minutes. Meanwhile, place the fresh chillies over the direct heat, turning them all the while until you have a nice char.

Drain the boiled veg and place back into the saucepan. Add the grilled chillies and the coriander. Using a stick blender, blitz all the ingredients until smooth. Finish with the lime and pickle juice, and season with a handsome pinch of salt, pepper and ancho chilli powder. Mix again and you are ready to serve.

This salsa goes great with tacos and burgers. Heck, it would taste amazing with chicken or a steak. I wouldn't put it in your coffee though. That probably wouldn't taste too good but you never can tell. Let me know if it works.

THANK YOU ★

This book is dedicated to my father, Ron Stevenson, and my three sons, Blue, Noah and Frasier. And major shout outs to my step-mom, Pam.

Special thanks to Chris Taylor (T-Bone Chops) who works tirelessly alongside me to cook, develop, write, drink beer and sing along to Foreigner! I couldn't have done this book without the knowledge and expertise of this gentle giant. Saying that, be careful hugging T-Bone, he doesn't know his own strength. Actually, forget the 'gentle giant' assessment, the dude is always hurting me with his love. Wow, that sounds wrong. Okay, I'll get on with the rest of the thank yous.

Matt Williams has been integral to everything we do. He makes our charcoal and sources the wood. Matt is the firebox manager and conjurer of all things that require fire.

David Loftus!!! You rule beyond ruling. Thanks for being so ding dong dang badass with your camera and lovely demeanour. And thanks to Ange Loftus for her creativity on the shoots, plus Jon Thompson and Gill from Sytch Farm Studios for the beautiful plates.

Zena Alkayat — my amazing and super patient editor. And the rest of the Quadrille team, including Emily Lapworth (for design), Sarah Chatwin (for copyediting), and everyone in publicity and sales.

Nathan, Ruth and Zoe Mills from The Butchery for supplying the best meat on the planet. Franco Lubini from Natoora for supplying next level fruit and veg. And Jan from The Flour Station for the amazing bread. How good does that burger look?

PRS (People's Republic of Sydenham)
There have been two couples that have come into my life in the past few years and they've become family: Matthew Clark, Bean, Tom Cundall, and Maddie Schofield.

Big thanks to the BBQ Zoo who are my companions throughout the summer on the festival circuit and show up in the book!
Chris Taylor
Matt Williams
Johnny Boots
Dave Fennings
Bryony Morganna
Martin Goodyear
Carl Brooks
Sam Jones
Olivier Guetdown
Nick Weston
Rama Basilio (Ramalamadingdong)
Magdalena Katsaros
Matt Burgess

Support crew, Suppliers and Sponsors
Gorilla Marketing and Events and Andy Gregorek for building the Truck and looking after our kit
Nick, Clare, and Marley Weston (Hunter Gather Cook)
Beth, Chris, Avery and Noelle Lee, Ruby
My awesome manager, Nicole Campbell, who looks after everything
A huge thanks to Jamie Oliver and the Food Tube family – I wouldn't be here without your support
Renault for building the ultimate cateratainment truck
Hellman's for the awesome sauces and for supporting me
The Unity Lager Crew! Ross, Will and Matty! Coalition Brewery!
Anton and the Maldon Salt family
Amar, Caroline, Mike and the Billings Sydenham Family
Netherton Foundry family
Alex Weller and the Patagonia crew
Ben Lang
Halldor Helgason and the Atrip Family
Weber UK

Drumbecue
Chris Acres
Hobbs House Bakery and the Herbert family… Please adopt me! I want to be a Herbert!
Dom Smales and the Gleam team

My best bros
Toby Millage and Trine (Indy & Otis)
Elliott Chaffer (Zephyr & Oshy)
Adam Kaleta and Emily (Karter & Zadie)
Matthew Clark (Black Canary Rye)
Geoff Glendenning
Wayne Yates

Festival Friends
Jimmy and Caela Doherty; Mat Kemp (Meatopia); Alex James and the Big Feastival family (watch out for Geronimo); Rob Da Bank, Gemma Thorogood and the Camp Bestival crew; Home Team BBQ: Madison Ruckel, Aaron Siegel, Reid Stone and the crew; Ben and Jon from Grillstock; Speed Machine Crew!

Friends, Musicians, Chefs and Artisans
Niall Davidson and Colin McSherry (Nuala); James Verity and the Superfantastic Crew; Rodney Bryant; Tim Woolcott; Jack, Megan and the Bibbo clan; Car Seat Headrest; Will Cheaney; James Wilson; Giles Coren; Fingal Ferguson; Joel Blacksmith; Henry Evans; Neil Rankin; Nick Solares; Nathan Outlaw; Ana Rita Valerio; Angie Mar; Tyson Ho; Nieves Barragán Mohacho; Jase Fleming; Kim Somauroo; Charlie Clapp; Liz Norris; Rich Herd; Zoe Collins; Tim Warwood; Adam Gendle; Sam and Asa Sims; Wise Buddah; Andy Latimer; Andy Slow & Low; Blues Kitchen; Jamie Eames; Tom Reader; Jamie Squibb; Sabrina Ghayour; Violent Soho; Johno Verity; Hersha Patel; Matt Barr; Strawberry Fields Farm: Sarah Crow and family; Andy Allen; Kerrie Hall; David Cramer, Jade Webb, Peter Brady and everyone at Blinkhorns; Henry Halonen; Dom Prosser; Graeme Hawkins; Brian Newton; Chris Allum (cheers for the use of your car for the book); and Dinosaur Jr for writing one of the best albums ever, Green Mind!

INDEX

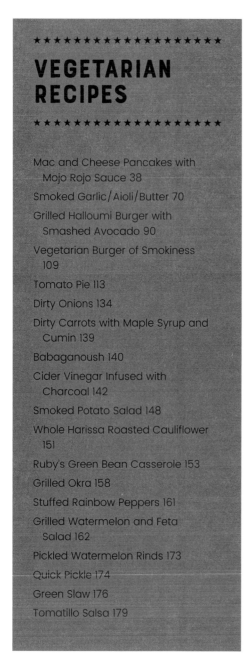

★ ★

PUBLISHING DIRECTOR Sarah Lavelle
COMMISSIONING EDITOR Zena Alkayat
HOME ECONOMIST Chris Taylor
CREATIVE DIRECTOR Helen Lewis
DESIGNER Emily Lapworth
FRONT COVER DESIGN Superfantastic
PHOTOGRAPHER David Loftus
PROPS STYLIST Ange Loftus
PRODUCTION DIRECTOR Vincent Smith
PRODUCTION CONTROLLER Nikolaus Ginelli

★ ★

Published in 2018 by Quadrille,
an imprint of Hardie Grant Publishing

Quadrille
52–54 Southwark Street
London SE1 1UN
quadrille.com

Cataloguing in Publication Data: a catalogue record for
this book is available from the British Library.

Reprinted in 2018, 2020 (twice), 2021
10 9 8 7 6 5

ISBN 978-1-78713-154-5

Printed in China

FSC
www.fsc.org
MIX
Paper from
responsible sources
FSC™ C020056